COMMUNICATING WITH *KI*
THE "SPIRIT" IN JAPANESE IDIOMS

Jeff Garrison and Kayoko Kimiya

KODANSHA INTERNATIONAL
Tokyo • New York • London

Distributed in the United States by Kodansha America, Inc.,
114 Fifth Avenue, New York, N.Y. 10011, and in the United
Kingdom and continental Europe by Kodansha Europe Ltd.,
95 Aldwych, London WC2B 4JF. Published by Kodansha
International Ltd., 17-14 Otowa 1-chome, Bunkyo-ku, Tokyo
112, and Kodansha America, Inc.

94 95 96 10 9 8 7 6 5 4 3 2 1

ISBN 4-7700-1833-9

Contents

Preface

This book is born of the belief that one important measure of fluency in a foreign language is the free and natural use of its idiomatic expressions in conversation, and that as many examples and as much pertinent information as possible should be bundled together in the presentation of any given word or phrase—which particles, words, and phrases it most commonly appears with, what related expressions there are and how they differ in nuance or usage. All this, it is believed, will greatly assist the serious student of language in mastering any such new linguistic structure. But, now, don't let that stop you from reading the book!

Why *Ki?*

We could go through a lot of pseudo-intellectual rigmarole about the early Taoist cult of longevity and neo-Confucian cosmology to justify our little book on *ki*—in fact we will do just that a little later—but basically, we decided *ki* deserved a book of its own when one of the authors picked up Maxi Priest's 1992 release *For Real* on Charisma Records and noticed it was subtitled *Honki* (本気) in Japanese. We knew right then and there that we had tapped into something big. If a hot young Jamaican reggae-rock artist was brandishing it on his album cover, *ki* just had to be *de rigueur*.

Be that as it may, our arm-twisting editors at Kodansha International, Michael Brase and Shigeyoshi Suzuki, forced us to come up with a *real* reason for writing the book, so we began casting about in the language to determine whether *ki* actually did warrant a book-length presentation. Our answer is in your hands. We found *ki* everywhere, in hundreds of common idioms and compounds. We found it on the front-page screamers of national newspapers and the trembling lips of tearful actresses on daytime

7

TV. We found it in practically every conversation either of us ever entered into or eavesdropped on, whether on crowded commuter trains or in smoky bars. We found, in short, that whenever Japanese talk about themselves or others, discuss human relations, or express their emotions, feelings, intentions or opinions, there was *ki* in abundance.

Dictionaries, large and small alike, confirmed this. Roughly speaking, we found *ki* to have some dozen definitions ranging from the sublime: the human spirit, *élan vital* or will to live; heart or mind; temperament or disposition; volition or intention; feelings or mood; consciousness, awareness, or sanity; emotion and sentiment; interest, concern, and attention—to the pedestrian: effervescence (what's lacking in beer when it's been sitting around too long, or missing in your life after forty), atmosphere (what you expect but most often find missing in Japanese restaurants when you're going out with your significant other), air (what you breathe once you're outside urban areas), and breath itself (which you're painfully out of by now if you're reading this sentence aloud). There was so much about *ki* that we had to decide which of its many meanings and uses to focus on. We settled on meanings revolving around mental or emotional states and activities because they were so common and so idiomatic. Conspicuous by their all-but-complete absence from this tome then are the words (and, to a lesser extent, the idioms) concerning air (*kūki* 空気 or empty *ki*), weather (*tenki* 天気 or heavenly *ki*,) and *brewski* (no kanji but lots of *ki*), although there was considerable debate regarding the fate of the last.

More about *Ki* than You Want—or Need—to Know

A necessarily brief look at the history of thinking on *ki—ch'i* in Chinese—shows that those Taoist philosophers and alchemists and Sung-dynasty neo-Confucians whom we gave such short shrift to earlier had some pretty definite thoughts on it. Their ruminations, while confounding translators (translations appearing in philosophical texts over the years range from "breath," "energy," "ether," "material force," "matter-energy," "nature," "passion" and "physical powers" to "vital breath," "vital force," "vital humors" and "vital power"), continue to occupy a central position in traditional Chinese thought on everything from metaphysics, ethics, and art to medicine, military strategy, politics, and sex.

Appearing early on in the appendix to the *Book of Changes* (*I Ching*), the *Analects* and other texts recorded hundreds of years before the birth of Christ, *ch'i* was originally written with the character 气 and regarded by ancient Chinese thinkers in much the same way as was *pneuma*, which originally meant "breath" in Greek and subsequently grew to be identified with the life principle or spirit by pre-Socratic natural philosophers of the Milesian school like Anaximenes. Early Taoists held that *ch'i* was an ethereal substance permeating the natural world as air, clouds, fog, and other gaseous vapors, as well as in the form of human breath. In constant flux, and found both within and without the human body—a view that has colored much oriental thinking on man and nature—*ch'i* grew to be considered a vital life force inhering in breath and bodily fluids which, when controlled and nurtured, could lead to great longevity, even immortality. Later *ch'i* was held to be the very cosmological stuff of all creation, generating heaven, earth, and man, while the appearance and demise of the myriad objects in the world were explained by the transformation of *ch'i* in its active and passive modes, *yin* 陰 and *yang* 陽 (*in* and *yō* in Japanese) or differentiation into five elements, wood, fire, earth, metal, and water, and the change, division, or combination thereof. Neo-Confucian Chu Hsi (1130–1200) described *ch'i* as the concrete, material, differentiating principle of things, which together with *li* (理) constitutes all beings, lending life to all things.

But, you say, we don't really give a hoot about any of that. All we want to know is what it means now and how to use it! We hear you. And to all those not-so-pedantic students of the language less impressed by the centuries of intellectual baggage carried by this wellspring of the Oriental spirit, for those more deeply roused by the simple observation that the word (and whatever it stands for) figures so prominently in daily Japanese conversation, for all those who marvel at the literally hundreds, if not thousands, of expressions scattered throughout the language in which it figures, we offer this book and remind you that were English like Japanese we would all owe a great linguistic debt to that mid-sixth-century B.C. Milesian philosopher Anaximenes and would, for example, be saying that "our pneuma is long" when we now say that we are patient, admonish our friends to "use their pneuma" when they hadn't sufficiently considered another's feelings, and "lose our pneuma" instead of fainting.

Mechanics

The more than 225 main entries, derivatives, and cognates chosen for inclusion here were selected based on their frequency of appearance in spoken and written Japanese and are organized in the traditional Japanese あいうえお fashion. The number of example sentences for any given idiom for the most part reflects its frequency of usage. Unless significant divergences in pronunciation or meaning are seen to exist, linguistically related words and idioms are generally collected under the most common idiom in the group: *ki o yasumeru* and *kiyasume* are found under *ki ga yasumaru,* and *tanki na* is found under *ki ga mijikai.* An index of words and idioms at the back of the book is provided to simplify a search for a specific term. In the text itself the following symbols have been used to indicate various types of information.

▬   Discussions of differentiations in usage.

➠   A variant or otherwise related expression included in an entry.

➤   Some related information or phrase, not sufficiently important or closely enough related to warrant its own entry.

☞   A synonym or related word or expression which is included in the book.

☛   An antonym included in the book.

⇨   A synonym not included in the book.

↔   An antonym not included in the book.

also   A variant pronunciation.

∗   Occasional glosses on vocabulary whose meaning is not immediately apparent from the English translation.

Communicating with *Ki*

iiki いい気 good *ki*

■ (be on) an ego trip, self-satisfaction, cockiness, conceit, vanity; (~ になる; ~ *ni naru*) let something go to one's head, think one is hot stuff ███

□ いい気になってると今にしっぺ返しされますよ。
Iiki ni natte 'ru to ima ni shippegaeshi saremasu yo.
Let your head get too big and they'll turn the tables on you real quick.

□ 親の気も知らないでまったくいい気なものだ。
Oya no ki mo shiranai de mattaku iiki na mono da.
You're so self-centered. Couldn't care less about your parents' feelings.

□ おとなしくしてりゃいい気になりやがって。
Otonashiku shite 'rya iiki ni nariyagatte.
Big man! Think your ███ doesn't stink, huh. / What are you gloating about, ███? (more literally, "If I keep quiet, you start acting big.")

Iiki is found almost exclusively in the two expressions appearing above: *iiki ni naru* and *iiki na mono*. Bear in mind that although the former is critical of a person's high estimation of himself, the latter, although critical, is less so and of a different character—being complacent or happy-go-lucky, especially when consideration of others is thought necessary, which is to say, almost all of the time in Japan. A synonym for *iiki ni naru* is *tengu ni naru* 天狗になる (lit., "become a flying goblin," from the long-nosed mythical monster's reputation for arrogance). One for *iiki na mono* is *nonki* 呑気. The latter is included in this book.

ikki 一気 one *ki*

■ all at once, at a stretch, in one shot, without stopping

□ 途中で休むとペースが崩れるから、一気にやってしまおう。
Tochū de yasumu to pēsu ga kuzureru kara, ikki ni yatte shimaō.
We're gonna lose momentum if we take a break, so let's just forge ahead and finish it up.

❏ おなかが減っていたので弁当を一気に食べたら、どんな味か分からなかった。

Onaka ga hette ita no de bentō o ikki ni tabetara, donna aji ka waka-ranakatta.

I was so famished I wolfed (scarfed) down my lunch without even tasting it.

❏ 一気、一気、一気。

Ikki! Ikki! Ikki!

Chug it! Chug it! / Chugalug, chugalug!

In a full sentence, *ikki* appears exclusively with the article *ni* as *ikki ni*.

⇨ *hito-iki ni* ひと息に

➡ikki-nomi 一気飲み a one-*ki* drink

■ chug, chugalug, guzzle

❏ 毎年4月には若い人の一気飲みによる急性アルコール中毒が多い。

Mainen shigatsu ni wa wakai hito no ikki-nomi ni yoru kyūsei-arukōru-chūdoku ga ōi.

Every April lots of young people get acute alcohol poisoning from chugalugging.

The Japanese college student's favorite pastime, drinking, takes on heroic proportions as *ikki-nomi* during the early days of a new "academic" (I use the word loosely) year, when clubs, circles, and classes get together for parties, or *konpa*, at which the major activity, in addition to scouting out the new guys and gals, is consuming massive quantities of beer, often amid shouts of *ikki, ikki, ikki!* from other students still on their feet.

---

iyake ga sasu 嫌気が差す disagreeable *ki* gets in

■ be disgusted with, be up to here with; have had enough of

❏ 堂々めぐり*で結論が出ない会議には嫌気が差すもんね。

Dōdō-meguri de ketsuron ga denai kaigi ni wa iyake ga sasu mon ne.

Don't you get fed up with meetings where endless talk never leads to any conclusions?

   * *dōdō-meguri*: lit., to go repeatedly around a Buddhist temple as a ritual; to repeat something *ad nauseam*.

❏ 安月給に嫌気が差して、会社をやめた。

Yasu-gekkyū ni iyake ga sashite, kaisha o yameta.

I got sick and tired of being paid next to nothing, so I quit my job.
⇨ *iya ni naru* 嫌になる

iroke 色気 colored *ki*

1. sex appeal

❐ この女優さんはもう50を過ぎているのにまだまだ色気があるね。
Kono joyū-san wa mō gojū o sugite iru no ni mada mada iroke ga aru ne.
This actress may never see fifty again, but she's still a turn-on.

❐ 彼女は色気たっぷりの仕草で歩く。
Kanojo wa iroke tappuri no shigusa de aruku.
She's got one sexy walk. / She's got all these sexy (foxy) little moves when she walks.

❐ この俳優はこぼれるような色気で中年女性を魅了している。
Kono haiyū wa koboreru yō na iroke de chūnen-josei o miryō shite iru.
This actor's oozing with so much sex appeal that he sweeps middle-aged women off their feet.

While the original meaning of *iroke* appears to have been the sexual quality of a woman that arouses a man's interest, the definition has now been expanded to include the same sort of quality in a man by which he arouses interest in a woman. And though lexical legitimacy has yet to be bestowed upon gay use of the term, such use is common. Gender aside, it is plain and simple sex appeal.

2. [in the phrase *iroke nuki (no kai)*] woman

❐ 今日は色気抜きの会だから飲むだけが楽しみだ。
Kyō wa iroke-nuki no kai da kara nomu dake ga tanoshimi da.
No gals at the party today, so the only fun thing to do is drink.

❐ たまには色気抜きの飲み会もいいものだ。
Tama ni wa iroke-nuki no nomikai mo ii mono da.
A stag party's all right too sometimes.

Derivative from the first sense, the term as seen in the above expressions originally referred to the presence of women who, by profession, entertained men in drinking establishments—geisha or hostesses traditionally, so-called "companions" today. Later usage expanded to include female office workers who were—and, in less enlightened companies, still are—expected to wait on their male coworkers and bosses at office parties and the like. From the perspective of such hidebound males, a get-together with no female employees in attendance is still referred to as *iroke nuki no kai*. Contemporary sensitivities require that students of the language be aware that many now feel that this phrase is a form of sexual discrimination.

☞ onnakke 女気

3. desire (for), interest (in)

❐ この合併の話には先方も色気を示している。

Kono gappei no hanashi ni wa senpō mo iroke o shimeshite iru.

The other party is also showing interest in the merger, too.

❐ 上田選手もうちへの移籍に色気があるようだ。

Ueda-senshu mo uchi e no iseki ni iroke ga aru yō da.

Ueda seems to want to be traded to our team.

☞ *ki ga aru* 気がある

➥iroke yori kuike 色気より食い気 eating over colored *ki*

■ be more interested in food than sex, like food better than sex

❐ 彼は色気より食い気だから、当分恋人は無理だね。

Kare wa iroke yori kuike da kara, tōbun koibito wa muri da ne.

He's more interested in feeding his face than women, so it'll be a while before he finds himself a girl.

❐ うちの娘は色気より食い気で、友だちとの会話もどこのケーキ屋さんがおいしいかとかそんなことばかりだ。

Uchi no musume wa iroke yori kuike de, tomodachi to no kaiwa mo doko no kēkiya-san ga oishii ka to ka sonna koto bakari da.

My daughter's more interested in eating than she is in boys. All she and her friends ever talk about is stuff like where you can get good pastries.

When used about men, *iroke yori kuike* indicates the subject is more interested in eating—and by extension a woman who can cook—than he is in how good-looking a woman is. But when a woman is the subject, the expression can be interpreted two ways: either she is less interested in *attracting* men than she is in eating, or she is less interested in *attractive* men than eating. *Iroke yori kuike* is similar—by a slight stretch of the imagination—to *hana yori dango* 花より団子 (dumplings before flowers, or less literally, substance over appearance), but the latter is somewhat broader in scope, used to describe a general preference for things of substantive importance rather than beauty or appearance.

➥iroke-zuku 色気づく colored *ki* adheres

■ become interested in (awaken to) sex, start to notice boys (girls); become sexually attractive

❐ 一郎の奴、いつまでも子供だと思ってたが、そろそろ色気づいてきたかな。

Ichirō no yatsu, itsu made mo kodomo da to omotte 'ta ga, sorosoro iroke-zuite kita na.

I was beginning to think the sap would never rise in old Ichirō (good ol' Ichirō), but it looks like he's finally starting to get that gleam in his eye.

❐ 隣の娘はいつの間にか色気づいてきたなぁ。

Tonari no musume wa itsu-no-ma ni ka iroke-zuite kita nā.

The girl next door is really starting to fill out. / The girl next door has started taking an interest in boys all of a sudden.

Although yet to attain lexical respectability in the sense of a person, usually an adolescent woman, becoming sexually attractive, this meaning of *iroke-zuku* is common in speech. The translation in the immediately preceding example would be the meaning as understood by most native speakers of the language.

---

inki (na) 陰気(な) shadowy *ki*

1. (of a person's attitude, countenance or mood) blue, gloomy, long-faced, melancholy; (of a person's temperament or personality) brooding, lugubrious, morose, saturnine, sulky, sullen, taciturn

❐ 中村さんはいい人なのに第一印象が陰気だからずいぶん損をしている。

Nakamura-san wa ii hito na no ni daiichi-inshō ga inki da kara zuibun son o shite iru.

Nakamura's a nice guy, but on first impression he seems so sullen that people don't really appreciate him.

❐ そんな陰気な顔しないで、笑って、笑って。

Sonna inki na kao shinai de, waratte, waratte.

Wipe that hang-dog look off your face and try a smile.

☛ *yōki (na)* 陽気(な)

2. (of a place or its atmosphere) dark, depressing, dreary, gloomy

❐ 深刻な問題を取り上げているのに、決して陰気な作品ではない。

Shinkoku na mondai o toriagete iru no ni, kesshite inki na sakuhin de wa nai.

For all the seriousness of its subject matter, this work isn't a bit gloomy.

❐ この家は日当たりが悪くて少し陰気だね。

Kono ie wa hiatari ga warukute sukoshi inki da ne.
This house doesn't get much sun. It's a little too dreary for me.

uchiki (na) 内気(な) inner *ki*

■ private, keep to *oneself*, not outgoing, not very sociable, reserved, shy

❑ 友成くんは内気なので営業には向かない。
Tomonari-kun wa uchiki na no de eigyō ni wa mukanai.
Tomonari's so shy that he's just not cut out for sales. / Tomonari's not outgoing enough to make it as a salesman.

❑ 幸子さんは内気だからか美人なのに男の友だちがいない。
Sachiko-san wa uchiki da kara ka bijin na no ni otoko no tomodachi ga inai.
Maybe the reason Sachiko doesn't have any boyfriends, even though she's really pretty, is that she's not very social.

↔ *gaikō-teki (na)* 外向的(な), *shakō-teki (na)* 社交的(な)
⇨ *naikō-teki (na)* 内向的(な)

utsurigi (na) 移り気(な) moving *ki*

■ (noun) a caprice, whim; (adj.) capricious, changeable, fickle, whimsical, doesn't stick with anything for long

❑ 移り気な野中さんは今回5回目の転職をした。
Utsurigi na Nonaka-san wa konkai gokai-me no tenshoku o shita.
That Nonaka just can't seem to settle down. This makes the fifth time he's changed jobs.

❑ うちの娘は移り気で、次から次へ*とお稽古ごとを始めるがどれも
長続きしない。
Uchi no musume wa utsurigi de, tsugi kara tsugi e to okeiko-goto o haji-meru ga dore mo nagatsuzuki shinai.
My daughter's so changeable, always taking up some new hobby but never sticking with anything for long.

* *tsugi kara tsugi e*: (changing) from one thing to another, one after another (a set phrase).

❑ あんな移り気な男を信用するんじゃなかった。
Anna utsurigi na otoko o shin'yō suru n' ja nakatta.
I should have known better than to trust a fickle guy like him.

For comparison with *ki ga ōi*, see usage note under that entry.

☞ *ki ga ōi* 気が多い, *ki ga kawariyasui* 気が変わりやすい (example under *ki ga kawaru*)

uwaki 浮気 floating *ki*

■ an affair, a fling, hanky-panky, something on the side; cheating, two-timing, unfaithfulness, stepping out

❑ 父の浮気が母にばれて大騒ぎになった。

Chichi no uwaki ga haha ni barete ōsawagi ni natta.

The shit hit the fan when Mom found out about Dad having an affair.

❑ 浮気のつもりが本気になってしまって、とうとう妻とは離婚した。

Uwaki no tsumori ga honki ni natte shimatte, tōtō tsuma to wa rikon shita.

What started out as a casual affair turned out to be the real thing, and I ended up getting a divorce from my wife.

❑ 主人の浮気の相手と称する女が図々しく尋ねてきた。

Shujin no uwaki no aite to shō-suru onna ga zūzūshiku tazunete kita.

Some woman calling herself my husband's lover had the nerve to come to the house.

➡uwakippoi 浮気っぽい like floating *ki*

■ adulterous, cheating, two-timing; [usually of a man, not necessarily implying that he is an adulterer or cheater] have a roving eye

❑ 彼みたいに浮気っぽい人と一緒になると苦労するのは目に見えてる＊よ。

Kare mitai na uwakippoi hito to issho ni naru to kurō suru no wa me ni miete 'ru yo.

Anybody can see that you're going to have nothing but trouble if you hook up with a two-timer like him.

＊ *me ni mieru*: lit., to be seen by the eye; to be certain, obvious.

Uwakippoi, like its less common synonym *uwaki na*, may also, though only rarely, be used to mean "not sticking to one thing for any length of time." The consensus of the authors and our usage panelists (read "friends" here) is that *uwaki na* does not merit an entry, but we have chosen to include the following example of how it may be used.

➤ 浮気なマリ子は今の彼氏でもう8人目だよ。

Uwaki na Mariko wa ima no kareshi de mō hachinin-me da yo.

Mariko's so fickle that she's already on her eighth boyfriend.

☞ *ki ga ōi* 気が多い (#1)

➡uwaki suru 浮気する float *one's ki*

■ carry on (with), [of a man] get a little [nookie, pussy] on the side, have an extramarital relationship (with), two-time, step out (on)

❐ 夫は浮気するような人じゃありません。

Otto wa uwaki suru yō na hito ja arimasen.

My husband's not the kind to cheat. / My husband would never fool around on me.

❐ アンケートの結果、既婚者の半数以上が浮気したいと考えていることが分かった。

Ankēto no kekka, kikon-sha no hansū ijō ga uwaki shitai to kangaete iru koto ga wakatta.

The survey results showed that more than half of married men and women would like to have an affair.

Thanks in large measure to TV soaps, gossip shows, and weekly mags, *uwaki suru* appears to be on the way out. No, the nation's philanderers are not having second thoughts because of AIDS and staying at home in front of the boob tube with the kids to watch cartoons and eat popcorn; on the contrary, the activity itself has apparently become the *in* thing to do and now flourishes as perhaps never before. It's the word *uwaki suru* that people don't use any more. The media has found it necessary to rehabilitate a musty old noun in its stead, *furin* 不倫 (originally, unethical, immoral; by extension, an illicit sexual relationship), spiffed it up by appending *suru* to make it the *de rigueur* contemporary verb for that very special and now somehow almost respectable extracurricular activity. As with other artifices like *tabako suru* タバコする (do tobacco, hence "smoke") the jury is still out on whether the construction will remain in the language when its popularizers move on to something else.

⇨ *furin suru* 不倫する

oshige mo naku 惜し気もなく with no regretful *ki*

■ freely, generously, openhandedly; without regret, without a second thought, without looking back

❐ あのミュージシャンはコンサート収益の大部分を惜し気もなく自然保護団体に寄付するんだって。

Ano myūjishan wa konsāto shūeki no dai-bubun o oshige mo naku shizenhogo-dantai ni kifu suru n' datte.

They say that that musician generously donates most of the proceeds from his concerts to environmental organizations.

❐ 彼女は惜し気もなく湯水のように金を使います*よ。

Kanojo wa oshige mo naku yumizu no yō ni kane o tsukaimasu yo.

She's such a spendthrift, she goes through money like it grew on trees.

* *yumizu no yō ni tsukau*: lit., use like hot water (a set phrase).

❏ もう10年も使って古くなったから、惜し気もなく捨てられるさ。

Mō jūnen mo tsukatte furuku natta kara, oshige mo naku suterareru sa.

Ten years I used that old sucker. I won't even think twice about getting rid of it.

Found under its noun form (*oshige*) in traditional dictionaries, *oshige mo naku* is included here as an idiom since *oshige* is encountered almost exclusively in this form in both written and spoken Japanese.

☞ *kimae* (*yoku*) 気前(よく) (in the sense of "giving freely")

otokogi 男気 manly *ki*

■ machismo, manliness, masculinity; bravery; chivalry, gallantry

❏ 「男女」* みたいな人ばっかりだと思ってたけど、まだあんな男気がある人もいたのねえ。

"Otoko-onna" mitai na hito bakkari da to omotte 'ta kedo, mada anna otokogi ga aru hito mo ita no nē.

This he-man appeared just when I figured all that was left were a bunch of pansies. / Here I was thinking there weren't any real men left and then, look, here's Mr. Macho himself.

* *otoko-onna*: an effeminate man or a masculine woman.

❏ ここは一つ男気を出して、「うん」と言って下さいよ。

Koko wa hitotsu otokogi o dashite, "Un" to itte kudasai yo.

Now's the time to be a man and just say you'll do it.

Variously defined as "the self-sacrificial nature [of men] which lends itself to the service of the weak or less fortunate" and "a temperament free from self-interest and willing to help the weak," this prime candidate for politically correct revisionist exclusion from the language is much more clearly—and positively—defined than its feminine counterpart *onnakke* 女っ気, which, by the way, has little to do with the qualities thought to be common to women except as homemakers.

---

otonage (ga) nai 大人気(が)ない no adult *ki*

■ childish, infantile, juvenile, puerile, sophomoric

❏ いい年*をしてそんな大人気ないことを言うもんじゃない。

Ii toshi o shite sonna otonage nai koto o iu mon ja nai.

Why don't you start acting your age and stop being such a baby.

  * *ii toshi*: advanced in years or, simply, old enough to know better.

❐ まさかあんな大人気ない行動をとる人とは思わなかったよ。

Masaka anna otonage nai kōdō o toru hito to wa omowanakatta yo.

Who would have thought he could ever behave so childishly?

Of an adult's, not a child's, attitude, behavior, speech, or way of doing something. Incidentally, the kanji 大人気 can be read two ways, rendering entirely different meanings. Happily, the subject of this entry, *otonage (ga) nai*, appears in only that phrase and is often written 大人げ, making it quite easy to spot. The other reading, *dai-ninki*, is a simple superlative, appearing in many of the same phrases as does *ninki* (for more information on which, see below).

---

onnakke 女っ気 woman's *ki*

1. (of an object or place) a woman's touch

❐ 若い女の部屋にしては女っ気がないなあ。

Wakai onna no heya ni shite wa onnakke ga nai nā.

For a young woman's room, this place sure lacks a feminine touch.

❐ わが家は全く女っ気がなくて殺風景だね。

Wagaya wa mattaku onnakke ga nakute sappūkei da ne.

The old place is kind of stark now, without any of the warmth a woman would give it.

2. (of a man) a sign, feeling or sense that *someone* has a girlfriend or wife

❐ あの人のまわりには全く女っ気がない。

Ano hito no mawari ni wa mattaku onnakke ga nai.

There's no sign at all that he's got a girlfriend (wife, woman).

❐ 真面目な息子だが、あまりに女っ気がないのも親としては気がかりだ。

Majime na musuko da ga, amari ni onnakke ga nai no mo oya toshite wa kigakari da.

My son's serious enough, but as a parent I'm a little worried that there don't seem to be any women in his life.

The good news is that the word itself is not particularly sexist, characterizing women as meek and subservient. The bad news is that it is used almost exclusively in the phrase *onnakke ga nai* as something seen as absent, especially in the lives of men. Oh, and yes, Virginia, there is a masculine equivalent, *mutatis mutandis*, replete with all the loathsome sociocultural accoutrements of a male-dominated society. Check out *otokogi* 男気.

---

also *onnagi* 女気, *onnake* 女気
☞ *iroke* 色気 (meaning #2)

katagi 堅気 firm *ki*

■ [of a person] serious, straight; reliable; [of an occupation] real, regular, legitimate, legit

❑ 暴力団も昨今では堅気の世界のビジネスに参入してきた。
Bōryoku-dan mo sakkon de wa katagi no sekai no bijinesu ni sannyū shite kita.
Organized crime has recently begun to branch out into legitimate business undertakings.

❑ 早く堅気になって奥さんを安心させてあげなさい。
Hayaku katagi ni natte okusan o anshin sasete agenasai.
Why don't you hurry up and get a real job, man, so your wife can stop worrying.

❑ 暴力団員の更正の難しさを訴えても、堅気の人はほとんど関心を示さない。
Bōryokudan-in no kōsei no muzukashi-sa o uttaete mo, katagi no hito wa hotondo kanshin o shimesanai.
You can argue all you want about the difficulty of reforming gang members, but your average Joe Blow could hardly care less.

In contrast to the traditional, socially unacceptable gangland livelihoods, which include gambling, prostitution, and bar ownership or employment, *katagi* refers to the occupations, life-styles, or ways of living of those who walk the straight and narrow.

---

kawaige (ga) nai かわい気(が)ない without cute (charming) *ki*

■ without charm or cuteness; that's not very nice

❑ 顔は可愛いのに言うことは実にかわい気がないのさ。
Kao wa kawaii no ni iu koto wa jitsu ni kawaige ga nai no sa.
For such a good-looking chick there's sure nothing lovable about the way she talks.

❐ 素直に喜べばいいのに、かわい気のないやつだな。

Sunao ni yorokobeba ii no ni, kawaige no nai yatsu da na.

It'd sure be nice if you could just show some appreciation (show how much you like it), but, no, you've got to be a sourpuss.

Kawaige (ga) nai is used almost exclusively in the negative, describing a lack of charm that is unexpected or unseemly.

☞ *ki ga tsuyoi* 気が強い

ki 気 *ki*

This is the biggy. The idioms and patterns given below (ending with *ki o waruku suru,* p. 119) feature *ki* in an integral—and relative—role in which its meaning changes depending on what comes before it (i.e., when *ki* follows one of three types of modifier: the sentence-ending form of a verb, the sentence-ending form of an "*i*" adjective, or the "*na*" form of a "*na*" adjective) and after it. The most common structures in which *ki* so appears include ~ *ki ga aru,* ~ *ki ga suru,* ~ *ki da,* and ~ *ki ni naru,* the swung dash " ~ " representing the modifier which determines the meaning of *ki* in the pattern. Broadly speaking, there are two types of pattern.

The first type of modifier ends in the so-called "dictionary" form of a verb expressing some form of action. *Ki* in this case takes on such meanings as plan, intention or inclination. When the degree of certainty is high in this usage, *ki* is interchangeable with *yotei* 予定 or *keikaku* 計画.

The second type ends either in the "dictionary" form of a verb expressing a condition (examples of this type of verb include *wakaru, dekiru,* and *iru*); or in the past, present continuous (~ *te iru*), past continuous (~ *te ita*) tenses of a verb, or in an adjective. In this case, ~ *yō na* is usually found attached to the preceding part. Here, *ki* has the sense of "feeling" and may be replaced by *kibun* 気分.

In both of the above types, *kimochi* 気持ち may be considered a synonym and, with the exception of the ~ *ki ga suru* pattern, so may *tsumori.*

~ ki ga aru ～気がある the *ki* to do ~ exists

■ feel like, be interested in, be ready to, be up for, intend to, want to

❐ 結婚する気があるのかないのか、はっきりしてちょうだい。

Kekkon suru ki ga aru no ka nai no ka, hakkiri shite chōdai.

Come on, just make up your mind whether you want to get married or not.

❐ 就職する気があるんだったら、そろそろ活動しなくちゃだめだよ。

Shūshoku suru ki ga aru n' dattara, sorosoro katsudō shinakucha dame da yo.

If you're thinking about getting a job, you're going to have to get on the ball and start looking around pretty soon.

❒ 買う気があるなら値段の交渉してみたら？

Kau ki ga aru nara nedan no kōshō shite mitara?

If you're interested in buying, why don't you try to get them to come down on the price?

❒ ダイエットする気はあるんだけど、ついつい甘い物に手が出ちゃう のよね。

Daietto suru ki wa aru n' da kedo, tsuitsui amai mono ni te ga dechau no yo ne.

I want to diet, but I just can't seem to stay away from (keep my hands off) the sweets.

Attached to the dictionary form of the verb, ~ *suru ki ga aru* expresses a present desire or intention to do something. The related expression ~ *ki ni naru* (〜気になる) suggests that a change from a previous state has resulted in the desire or intention to do something. ~ *Ki ga aru* is often replaced by ~ *ki da*. In the first three of the above four examples, ~ *suru ki ga aru* and ~ *suru ki ni naru* are interchangeable; in the fourth they remain interchangeable but ~ *ki da* imparts a firmer sense of resolve to drop a few pounds. While ~ *ki ga aru* implies that there are several possible courses of action from which a particular one has been chosen, ~ *ki da* implies that either none exist or at least that they are not considered viable alternatives.

☞ ~ *ki ni naru* 〜気になる (see under *ki ni naru* 気になる), ~ *ki da* 〜 気だ (subentries under this entry)

☛ ~ *ki ga aru* 〜気がある

➡~ ki ga okoru 〜気が起こる the *ki* to do ~ happens

■ get in the mood to do, bring oneself to do

❒ 原稿を書く気が起こるまでしばらくテレビゲームでもやろうっと。

Genkō o kaku ki ga okoru made shibaraku terebigēmu de mo yarō tto.

Maybe I ought to play a video game for a while until I get in the mood to start working on the manuscript.

❒ あまりのことに泣く気も起こらなかった。

Amari no koto ni naku ki mo okoranakatta.

Things were so terrible that I couldn't even cry.

❒ コーチに馬鹿にされて猛烈に練習する気が起こった。

Kōchi ni baka ni sarete mōretsu ni renshū suru ki ga okotta.

I went all out in practice when the coach made fun of me.

☞ ~ *ki ni naru* 気になる (see subentry under this entry)

➡~ ki ga shinai 〜気がしない

1. don't feel (like doing)

❑ あれ以来、もう何もする気がしないのさ。

Are irai, mō nani mo suru ki ga shinai no sa.

Ever since, I just haven't felt like doing anything.

❑ いくら勧められてもそんな物は買う気が全然しないよ。

Ikura susumerarete mo sonna mono wa kau ki ga zenzen shinai yo.

Doesn't matter how hard they try to persuade me, I'm not at all interested in buying anything like that.

❑ やめた、やめた、食う気しない。

Yameta, yameta, kuu ki shinai.

Nope, I've changed my mind. I don't feel like eating anymore.

Beware—the antonym of ~ *ki ga shinai* is not ~ *ki ga suru*.

☞ ~ *ki ni naranai* 〜気にならない (examples under ~ *ki ni naru* 〜気になる)

☛ ~ *ki ni naru* 〜気になる (see subentry under this entry)

2. don't feel, don't get the feeling, don't think

❑ 彼はほめているつもりだろうが、あれではほめられている気がしないさ。

Kare wa homete iru tsumori darō ga, are de wa homerarete iru ki ga shinai sa.

He may think it's a compliment, but it sure doesn't feel that way.

❑ あんな少しじゃ飲んだ気がしねえ。もう1軒行こうぜ。

Anna sukoshi ja nonda ki ga shinē. Mō ikken ikō ze.

You call that drinkin'? I haven't even got a buzz, man. Whaddya say we hit another bar.

While *taberu ki ga shinai* 食べる気がしない means the same as *tabe-taku nai* 食べたくない, namely that one does not want to eat; *tabeta ki ga shinai* 食べた気がしない means something akin to "that was so bad (such a small amount, etc.) that I don't feel that I've eaten at all."

☛ ~ *ki ga suru* 〜気がする (see subentry under this entry)

➡~ ki ga suru 〜気がする the *ki* to do ~ does

■ believe, feel (like), get the notion (that), think

❑ 君とならうまくやっていけそうな気がするんだ。

Kimi to nara umaku yatte ikesō na ki ga suru n' da.

I get the feeling that you and I are going to do just fine together.

❑ 熱がありそうな気がする。学校は休もうかな。

Netsu ga arisō na ki ga suru. Gakkō wa yasumō ka na.

I feel kinda like I've got a fever. Maybe I ought to cut (skip) school today.

❏ 彼の言い分も分かる気がするが、やはり賛成できない。

Kare no iibun mo wakaru ki ga suru ga, yahari sansei dekinai.

I think I understand what he's saying, but I just can't go along with it.

❏ たかが一泊旅行にこんな大きな荷物持って行くのはカッコ悪い気がする。

Takaga ippaku ryokō ni konna ōki na nimotsu motte iku no wa kakko warui ki ga suru.

I get the feeling (it strikes me) that taking a big suitcase like this on a little overnighter is gonna look pretty stupid.

❏ ちょっと覗いてみたい気もするなあ。

Chotto nozoite mitai ki mo suru nā.

You know, I'd kinda like to take a peek.

❏ この人から離れられなくなってしまうような気がした。

Kono hito kara hanarerarenaku natte shimau yō na ki ga shita.

I felt like I might not be able to go back to a life without him.

❏ あの人にはどこかで会ったような気がするんだが、どこだったか思い出せない。

Ano hito ni wa doko ka de atta yō na ki ga suru n' da ga, doko datta ka omoidasenai.

I've got the feeling that I've met him somewhere before, but I can't remember where.

❏ ちょっと路地を入っただけで戦前の東京に迷い込んだような気がした。

Chotto roji o haitta dake de senzen no Tōkyō ni mayoikonda yō na ki ga shita.

I felt like I had stepped back in time to prewar Tokyo almost as soon as I got on the back streets.

Less definite than ~ *to omou*, ~ *ki ga suru* is a somewhat evasive way of saying what you think. That is, it is an artful—some would say typically Japanese—way of avoiding responsibility for suggesting an idea or a strong commitment to one. Add *yō na*, as in *yō na ki ga suru*, and you're practically a seasoned politician who is just impossible to pin down. While *yō na* can be appended to any usage of *ki ga suru*, it is especially recommended when the word preceding the expression is any part of speech other than an adjectival verb 形容動詞 to make the expression more natural. This may arise from basing one's comments on something only dimly remembered. Finally, the negative of *ki ga suru*, *ki ga shinai* (which see) appears to be seldom used when the future is being spoken of.

➥ ~ ki ga deru 〜気が出る the *ki* to do ~ comes out

■ want to do, feel like doing

❏ 勉強する気が出るように、お父さんからも話してやって下さいな。

Benkyō suru ki ga deru yō ni, otōsan kara mo hanashite yatte kudasai na.

You have a talk with him too, Father, and see if you can't motivate (get) him to study.

❏ 彼も失業保険が切れそうになってやっと仕事を探す気が出てきたようだね。

Kare mo shitsugyō-hoken ga kiresō ni natte yatto shigoto o sagasu ki ga dete kita yō da ne.

What with his unemployment benefits coming to an end, it seems he's finally decided to look for a job.

➥ ~ ki ga nai 〜気がない the *ki* to do ~ doesn't exist

■ not be ready to, be unready to, don't feel like, don't intend to

❏ 買う気がないのに冷やかしたのかい。

Kau ki ga nai no ni hiyakashita no kai.

What did you do, just go around window shopping and pestering the clerks even though you never intended to buy anything?

❏ 借りる気はなかったが、一応比較のためにアパートを見せてもらうことにした。

Kariru ki wa nakatta ga, ichiō hikaku no tame ni apāto o misete morau koto ni shita.

I had no intention of renting the apartment, but I had them show it to me anyway for the sake of comparison.

☛ ~ ki ga aru 〜気がある

➥ ~ ki da 〜気だ *ki* is

1. be going to, be inclined to, intend to, plan to

❏ 優勝できなかったら丸坊主になる気だ。

Yūshō dekinakattara marubōzu ni naru ki da.

I'm gonna shave my head if we don't win the championship.

❏ 大学へ行く気なら学費ぐらいはなんとかしてやるから頑張れ。

Daigaku e iku ki nara gakuhi gurai wa nan to ka shite yaru kara ganbare.

If you're planning to go to college, I'll do what I can to come up with the money for your tuition. Go for it.

❏ あいつ本当にカンニングする気らしいぜ。

Aitsu hontō ni kanningu suru ki rashii ze.

He really intends to cheat. / He's really gonna cheat.

❏ 今のところは参加する気でいますが、はっきりした返事はもうしばらくお待ち下さい。

Ima no tokoro wa sanka suru ki de imasu ga, hakkiri shita henji wa mō shibaraku omachi kudasai.

At the moment I'm inclined to take part, but please wait a little longer for my final decision.

☞ ~ *ki ga aru* 〜気がある (see subentry under same entry)

2. feel like, think like

❒ たった半年暮らしただけでその国のことがすべて分かったような気でいる。

Tatta hantoshi kurashita dake de sono kuni no koto ga subete wakatta yō na ki de iru.

I only lived there for six months, but I feel as though I got to know the country inside out.

❒ オーディションに受かっただけなのに、もう大女優になった気らしい。

Ōdishon ni ukatta dake na no ni, mō dai-joyū ni natta ki rashii.

She acting like she's a big movie star even though all she did was pass the audition.

❒ 清水の舞台から飛び降りた気で転職しましたよ。

Kiyomizu no butai kara tobiorita ki de tenshoku shimashita yo.

It was a big step for me to change jobs. / I felt I was jumping off the deep end when I changed jobs.

❒ 大船に乗った*気で、安心してお任せ下さい。

Ōbune ni notta ki de, anshin shite omakase kudasai.

Just relax, you're in safe hands. Leave everything to me.

　* *ōbune ni notta*: lit., ride on a big ship; a set phrase often followed by *yō de*.

❒ 催眠術にかかっている間は犬になった気でいたのかい。

Saimin-jutsu ni kakatte iru aida wa inu ni natta ki de ita no kai.

What, did you feel like you'd turned into a dog when you were under hypnosis?

☞ ~ *ki ni natta* 〜気になった、~ *ki ni natte iru* 〜気になっている (see ~ *ki ni naru* subentry under this entry)

➥~ ki ni saseru 〜気にさせる

■ make someone (want to) do something, convince someone to do something, bring someone around

❒ 「お子さんを勉強する気にさせるのはお母さんの役目ですよ」と言われた。

"Okosan o benkyō suru ki ni saseru no wa okāsan no yakume desu yo" to iwareta.

She told me, "It's a mother's job to make her children want to study."

❒ 弟を結婚する気にさせようと両親はいろんな手を使っている。

Otōto o kekkon suru ki ni saseyō to ryōshin wa ironna te o tsukatte iru.

My parents are pulling out all the stops to get my younger brother in the mood to marry.

➡ ~ ki ni naru 〜気になる

1. be (get) in the mood to do, feel like doing, want to do

❑ あまり興味がない分野の本も書評でほめてあると読んでみる気になる。

Amari kyōmi ga nai bunya no hon mo shohyō de homete aru to yonde miru ki ni naru.

I feel like reading books even in fields I'm not particular interested in when they've gotten good reviews.

❑ しばらくは未練もあったが、最近やっとあきらめる気になった。

Shibaraku wa miren mo atta ga, saikin yatto akirameru ki ni natta.

For a while there I just couldn't let go, but recently I've finally resigned myself to things.

❑ 人間、死ぬ気になれば何でも出来る。

Ningen, shinu ki ni nareba nan de mo dekiru.

Human beings can do anything if they go about it as if there was no tomorrow.

❑ 金山さんもやっと結婚する気になったらしいよ。

Kanayama-san mo yatto kekkon suru ki ni natta rashii yo.

It looks like Kanayama is finally warming up to the idea of getting married.

❑ いくらおいしいって言われても、生玉子だけは食べる気にならないんだ。

Ikura oishii tte iwarete mo, nama-tamago dake wa taberu ki ni naranai n' da.

Raw eggs are the one thing I can't bring myself to eat, no matter how good people say they are.

❑ 両親から顔を見るたびにうるさく言われるが、見合いをする気にはなれない。

Ryōshin kara kao o miru tabi ni urusaku iwareru ga, miai o suru ki ni wa narenai.

My parents bug me about it every time I see them, but I'm not into (I can't see) doing the arranged marriage thing.

The dictionary form of the verb in the above examples is often replaced by ~ *shiyō to iu* 〜しようという before *ki ni naru* with no significant change in meaning. Examples of this structure follow.

❑ 父が手術を受けようという気になってくれて私たちも一安心だ。

Chichi ga shujutsu o ukeyō to iu ki ni natte kurete watashi-tachi mo hito-anshin da.

Now that Dad's ready to have the operation, it's a big relief for the whole family.

❑ 真面目に働こうという気になりさえすれば、仕事はすぐ見つかるよ。

Majime ni hatarakō to iu ki ni nari sae sureba, shigoto wa sugu mitsukaru yo.

All you've got to do is get serious about working and you'll find a job right away.

❑ あの人を殺して自分も死のうという気になったこともあります。

Ano hito o koroshite jibun mo shinō to iu ki ni natta koto mo arimasu.

At one point I was all set to kill him and then die myself.

There is an important distinction—implied if not explicit in the original Japanese—between ~ *ki ga aru* 〜気がある, which is simply descriptive of one's present state of mind, and ~ *ki ni naru* 〜気になる, which implies that ones present thoughts on the topic of discussion are different from before.

☞ ~ *ki ga aru* 〜気がある, ~ *ki ga okoru* 〜気が起こる (see subentries under this entry)

2. feel like one has already done something when one hasn't

❑ 応募葉書を出しただけなのにもう抽選に当たった気になっている。

Ōbo-hagaki o dashita dake na no ni mō chūsen ni atatta ki ni natte iru.

I may have just mailed in the postcard, but I already feel like a winner.

❑ 旅行案内を読んで行った気になれるんだから、安上がりだね。

Ryokō annai o yonde itta ki ni nareru n' da kara, yasuagari da ne.

It's a cheap way to travel when you feel like you've already been there just from reading the travel brochure.

❑ パン屋さんでちょうど焼きたてのパンが買えると得したような気になるね。

Panya-san de chōdo yakitate no pan ga kaeru to toku-shita yō na ki ni naru ne.

You get the feeling that you've really lucked out when you go to a bakery and they've just put out the fresh stuff, don't you.

Similar to ~ *(yō na) ki ga suru* 〜(ような)気がする, the expressions are interchangeable in the three examples above without altering the meaning. While ~ *ki ga suru* 〜気がする is a straightforward description of one's present state of mind, however, *(shita yō na) ki ni naru* 〜気になる suggests a *fanciful* change in one's attitude or feeling, or that one's

present feelings on the topic of discussion are somehow different from
before.

---

kiai 気合い matching *ki*'s

■ backbone, fight, heart, spirit

❑ 若の富士の顔は気合いが入っていた。

Wakanofuji no kao wa kiai ga haitte ita.

One look at (the sumo wrestler) Wakanofuji's face and you could tell
that he was psyched up.

❑ 「気合いを入れろ」とコーチに発破をかけられた。

"Kiai o irero," to kōchi ni happa o kakerareta.

The coach fired me up (lit a fire under me) by yelling "Fight!"

❑ 気合いの足りない人間は若くてもダメだ。

Kiai no tarinai ningen wa wakakute mo dame da.

I don't care how young you are, you're no good to me without any get-
up-and-go.

kiou 気負う to take on *ki*

■ get into, get worked up, screw *oneself* up (to do *something*),
work *oneself* up

❑ 気負うのもいいが、過ぎると傲慢になるおそれがあるよ。

Kiou no mo ii ga, sugiru to gōman ni naru osore ga aru yo.

There's nothing wrong with psyching yourself up, but go too far and you
can end up trying to lord it over everybody.

❑ 俺が、俺が、と気負っていた昔が嘘のようだ。

Ore ga, ore ga, to kiotte ita mukashi ga uso no yō da.

Sometimes it doesn't seem possible the way I used to think I could do
just about anything.

➡kioi 気負い taking on *ki*

■ ardor, enthusiasm, fervor, intensity, zeal

❑ 彼には、うちの社は俺でもっているという気負いがある。

Kare ni wa, uchi no sha wa ore de motte iru to iu kioi ga aru.

He's worked himself up into thinking that the company couldn't get
along without him.

❑ 昔の日記は若さ故の気負いがあふれていて、読むのが面はゆいの
さ。

Mukashi no nikki wa wakasa yue no kioi ga afurete ite, yomu no ga omohayui no sa.

My old diaries are so full of the boundless enthusiasm of youth that it's kind of embarrassing to read them now.

❑ 気負いを捨てて肩の力を抜けば、楽になれるよ。

Kioi o sutete kata no chikara o nukeba, raku ni nareru yo.

Simmer down and relax, and things will smooth out a little.

kiokure (ga) suru 気後れ(が)する *one's ki* falls behind

■ lose *one's* nerve, back down, back out, chicken out, cop out

❑ あなたは気後れするようには見えないが、意外ですね。

Anata wa kiokure suru yō ni wa mienai ga, igai desu ne.

I sure never figured you for the type to get cold feet.

❑ 準備はしていたが、いざとなると気後れがして何も言えなかった。

Junbi wa shite ita ga, iza to naru to kiokure ga shite nani mo ienakatta.

I was all prepared, but I chickened out when the chips were down and couldn't get a word out.

❑ あなたの方が正しいのだから、気後れしないで堂々としていなさい。

Anata no hō ga tadashii no da kara, kiokure shinai de dōdō to shite inasai.

You're the one who's right, so don't back down now. Give 'em hell.

ki ga au 気が合う *ki's* match

■ get along (well); be compatible, like-minded, on the same wave length; hit it off

❑ あの人とは最初に紹介されたときから気が合う。

Ano hito to wa saisho ni shōkai sareta toki kara ki ga au.

He and I've hit it off ever since we were first introduced.

❑ どうせ飲むなら、会社の上司とじゃなくて気の合う者同士で行きたいよ。

Dōse nomu nara, kaisha no jōshi to ja nakute ki no au mono dōshi de ikitai yo.

If I've got to go out drinking, I'd sure rather do it with people I get along with instead of my boss.

❑ 山田さんはいい人だとは思うんだけど、なぜか気が合わない。

Yamada-san wa ii hito da to wa omou n' da kedo, naze ka ki ga awanai.

I'm sure Yamada is a fine person, but the chemistry is just not right for us.

Expresses the sympathetic feelings between like-minded individuals rather than agreement among them on any particular matter.

⇨ *uma ga au* 馬が合う

ki ga arai 気が荒い *ki* is rough

■ temperamental, excitable, volcanic

❏ ある程度気が荒い馬でないとよい競走馬にはならないそうだ。

Aru teido ki ga arai uma de nai to yoi kyōsō-ba ni wa naranai sō da.

They say an animal has got to be somewhat temperamental to make a good racehorse.

❏ 気が荒い人が多い職場なので、けんかが絶えない。

Ki ga arai hito ga ōi shokuba na no de, kenka ga taenai.

There're so many contentious people where I work that there's no end to the arguing.

↔ *odayaka na* おだやかな, *otonashii* おとなしい

ki ga aru 気がある there is *ki*

■ be interested in, take to, have a place in *one's* heart for, be keen on, take a fancy to

❏ この話には十分気があるんだが、いろいろとこちらにも事情があってねえ。

Kono hanashi ni wa jūbun ki ga aru n' da ga, iroiro to kochira ni mo jijō ga atte nē.

We're interested enough in the project; it's just that you have to realize that there are other considerations involved for us here.

❏ 今度の縁談には十分気があるんだ。

Kondo no endan ni wa jūbun ki ga aru n' da.

She's very interested in the latest marriage proposal.

❏ あいつはどうやら昭子さんに気があるらしいが、彼女の方は全然あいつに気のある素振りは見せない。

Aitsu wa dō yara Akiko-san ni ki ga aru rashii ga, kanojo no hō wa zenzen aitsu ni ki no aru soburi wa misenai.

It looks like he's got the hots for Akiko all right, but she's showing no signs that she even knows he's alive.

While ~ *ni ki ga aru* means to be interested in something, as does the expression ~ *ni kyōmi ga aru*, unlike the latter it connotes a sometimes strong desire for the object of affection—usually someone or something of sexual or financial interest—rather than a passing or dispassionate interest. You would use the expression ~ *ni kyōmi ga aru* if you were interested in soccer, or following a particular athlete's career as a sports commentator, while you would use ~ *ni ki ga aru* about that same athlete if you were you bent on luring him to play for your team or going out on a date with him. This idiom, by the way, should not be confused with ~ *ki ga aru* preceded by the dictionary form of a verb and exemplified under the *ki* entry.

☛ *ki ga nai* 気がない

ki ga ii 気がいい *ki* is good

■ amiable, good-hearted, good-natured, have a good disposition, pleasant; laid-back

❐ 彼は気がいいからまわりの人にずいぶんと利用されている。

Kare wa ki ga ii kara mawari no hito ni zuibun to riyō-sarete iru.

He's such an easygoing guy (a big softie, a pussycat) that he's always letting people take advantage of him.

❐ 息子は気がよすぎて人に頼まれたことは断れないので、将来が心配だ。

Musuko wa ki ga yosugite hito ni tanomareta koto wa kotowarenai no de shōrai ga shinpai da.

I'm worried about my son's future because he's just too nice (softhearted) for his own good. He can't say no when someone asks him to do something.

❐ タローは気のいい犬で、猫に餌を横取りされても怒らない。

Tarō wa ki no ii inu de, neko ni esa o yokodori sarete mo okoranai.

Taro's such a good-natured dog that he doesn't even get mad when some cat snatches his food away.

➡ki no ii hito 気のいい人 a person with good *ki*

■ an amiable person, a good person, a personable person, a person with a good disposition

❐ 厚さんのように気のいい人は珍しいですよ。

Atsushi-san no yō ni ki no ii hito wa mezurashii desu yo.

People as good-natured as Atsushi are rare.

❐ 彼は気のいい人で決して他人の言うことを悪くとらない。

Kare wa ki no ii hito de kesshite tanin no iu koto o waruku toranai.

He's such a prince that he'd never take anything the wrong way.

⇨ *hito ga ii* 人がいい [Used, obviously, only about people.]

ki ga ōi 気が多い　there is a lot of *ki*

1. like to play the field, like the ladies (men), be flirtatious; be fickle

❑ あいつ今3人の女性とつきあってるらしいよ。相変わらず気が多いな。

Aitsu ima sannin no josei to tsukiatte 'ru rashii yo. Aikawarazu ki ga ōi na.

Man's in his usual fine form, going out with three chicks at the same time.

❑ おとなしそうな顔して、あんな気の多い女とは知らなかった。俺、くやしいよ。

Otonashisō na kao shite, anna ki no ōi onna to wa shiranakatta. Ore, kuyashii yo.

She looked like such a quiet girl, how was I to know she'd be screwing around on me. Jeez, that pisses me off.

　　☞ *uwakippoi* 浮気っぽい and *uwaki (na)* 浮気(な) (both under *uwaki* 浮気)

2. want to do everything (a lot of things), capricious, have a lot of irons in the fire, [～多すぎて] spread *oneself* (a little) thin

❑ 娘が就職活動中なんだが、結構気が多くてなかなか決まらないんだ。

Musume ga shūshoku katsudō-chū nan da ga, kekkō ki ga ōkute naka-naka kimaranai n' da.

My daughter's looking for a job right now, but there are so many things she wants to do she just can't seem to make up her mind.

❑ 彼は気が多くていろんな趣味を持っている。

Kare wa ki ga ōkute ironna shumi o motte iru.

He's an inquisitive guy with a lot of hobbies.

Similar to *utsurigi (na)* 移り気(な), but while *utsurigi (na)* indicates that the person is always flitting from one thing or person to another, *ki ga ōi* suggests that several interests (flames?) hold the person's attention at the same time.

---

ki ga ōkiku naru 気が大きくなる *ki* grows large

■ be (feel) expansive, flushed, uninhibited; let it all hang out; don't sweat the small stuff (shit)

❏ 酔うと気が大きくなってできもしない事を約束する癖がある。

You to ki ga ōkiku natte deki mo shinai koto o yakusoku suru kuse ga aru.

Every time I tie one on I start feeling my oats and go around making all kinds of promises that I can't deliver on.

❏ 宝くじが当たったので気が大きくなってやたら買い物しまくったら足が出てしまった。

Takarakuji ga atatta no de ki ga ōkiku natte yatara kaimono shimakut-tara ashi ga dete shimatta.

In a liberal mood after winning the lottery, I went on a shopping spree and blew all the money I'd won, and then some.

ki ga okenai 気が置けない unable to place *ki*

■ feel at ease (with *someone*), easy to be around; [of a situation] informal, relaxed

❏ 気が置けない友人と飲むのが一番のストレス解消法だよ。

Ki ga okenai yūjin to nomu no ga ichiban no sutoresu kaishō-hō da yo.

Having a drink with a friend you can open up to is the best way I know to unwind.

❏ こういう気の置けない会だと時間のたつのが早いね。

Kō iu ki no okenai kai da to jikan no tatsu no ga hayai ne.

Time really flies at get-togethers like this.

❏ 彼女は気の置けない人だからお友達も多いらしいわ。

Kanojo wa ki no okenai hito da kara otomodachi mo ōi rashii wa.

She's so easy to talk to that she's got lots of friends.

A contemporary example of how language may change to take on an opposite meaning, usage of *ki no okenai hito* among young people seems to indicate a misconstruction of its meaning, possibly due to the *okenai* element, "unable to place," taken to imply that the person in question is unworthy of trust; that is, that one shouldn't *place* one's *ki* in him or her. Though it is still too early for this recent trend to enjoy lexicographic respectability, the trend bears watching. Students of the language should be aware that although both meanings are in use, only the original is widely accepted.

---

ki ga omoi 気が重い *ki* is heavy

■ be (feel) blue, bummed-(out), down, low heavy-hearted

❐ 19日までにあと15も例文を作らなければならないので気が重い。

Jūku-nichi made ni ato jūgo mo reibun o tsukuranakereba naranai no de ki ga omoi.

It's depressing to think that I've got to come up with fifteen more example sentences by the nineteenth.

❐ 仕事とはいえ結果的にはあの人を裏切ることになると思うと気が重い。

Shigoto to wa ie kekka-teki ni wa ano hito o uragiru koto ni naru to omou to ki ga omoi.

I know it comes with the job, but it makes me feel bad to think that it amounts to stabbing him in the back.

Used of the way one feels when facing a disagreeable situation or distasteful task rather than of an emotional state resulting from some unpleasant event, past or present. The latter meaning is more appropriately expressed with either *ki ga shizumu* 気が沈む or *ki ga meiru* 気が滅入る, both of which are included herein.

☞ *ki ga shizumu* 気が沈む, *ki ga meiru* 気が滅入る
☛ *ki ga karui* 気が軽い

ki ga katsu 気が勝つ *ki* is victorious

■ hard-nosed, opinionated, spirited, strong-minded, strong-willed, unyielding

❐ 気が勝った人で、ひとから注意されると猛烈に反発するんだよ。

Ki ga katta hito de, hito kara chūi sareru to mōretsu ni hanpatsu suru n' da yo.

A strong-willed woman, she'll jump on anybody who tries to give her advice.

❐ 姉貴は気が勝ってて絶対弱音は吐かないんだ。

Aneki wa ki ga katte 'te zettai yowane wa hakanai n' da.

My big sister's a real competitor. No way she'll ever give up. / My big sister is her own woman. You won't hear her moaning and groaning about anything.

Used only in the ~ *katta* or ~ *katte iru* forms, often (though not always) disparagingly of a woman who "doesn't know her place," i.e., one who has her own opinions and is unwilling to go along with what a man tells her.

---

kachiki (na) 勝ち気(な) victorious *ki*

■ feisty, competitive, hates to lose, strong-minded, strong-willed, tough

❒ 勝ち気な性分で、いつもトップを走っていないと気が済まない。
Kachiki na shōbun de, itsumo toppu o hashitte inai to ki ga sumanai.
She's so competitive that she's got to be right up there at the top or she's not satisfied.

❒ 子供の時から勝ち気で負けず嫌いだったしさ。
Kodomo no toki kara kachiki de makezu-girai datta shi sa.
She's been like that since she was a kid, just hated to lose.

Of a person, usually a woman or child, who will do just about anything not to end up on the losing side in an argument. Regularly used disparagingly or with minimal, grudging approval of a woman who refuses to knuckle under to a man.

☞ *ki ga tsuyoi* 気が強い
⇨ *kikanu ki* 利かぬ気, *kikanki* きかん気 (used exclusively of children)

---

ki ga karui 気が軽い *ki* is light

■ feel light-hearted, relieved, feel like a load has been lifted from *one's* shoulders

❒ 今月のノルマが達成できてしばらくは気が軽い。
Kongetsu no noruma ga tassei dekite shibaraku wa ki ga karui.
I'm gonna be walking on air now that I've made my quota for this month. / What a load off my mind it is to have met my quota this month.

❒ とりあえず第二志望の学校に受かったので気が軽くなった。
Toriaezu daini-shibō no gakkō ni ukatta no de ki ga karuku natta.
Knowing that I've at least made it into my second-choice school is a big relief.

Ki ga karui is used to describe a feeling of light-heartedness which is normally the result of some felicitous event or state of affairs in the past. Such being the case, it differs somewhat in usage from its most obvious antonym *ki ga omoi*, which looks forward—literally—to the ominous future for its referent. *Ki ga karuku naru* is also to be distinguished from its near synonym *ki ga hareru* in that the former describes a feeling of relief upon completion of some duty or distasteful task such as work or study, while the latter results more from a clearing of the air and return to normalcy after that anxious moment when you were sure the teacher spotted your crib sheet or after the prolonged gloom of a languid stock market has suddenly lifted.

☞ *ki ga omoi* 気が重い

kigaru (na)　気軽(な)　light *ki*

■ be easy-going, laid-back; lighthearted

❑ 結婚とかなんとか難しいこと言わないで、気軽なつきあいをしようよ。

Kekkon to ka nan to ka muzukashii koto iwanai de, kigaru na tsukiai o shiyō yo.

Come on now, don't get all uptight about gettin' married and stuff. Let's just have a good time together.

❑ 遠慮なく気軽に遊びに来てくださいね。

Enryo naku kigaru ni asobi ni kite kudasai ne.

Don't hesitate to just drop by some time when you're in the mood.

❑ 栄養たっぷりでしかも気軽に作れるメニューをご紹介しましょう。

Eiyō tappuri de shikamo kigaru ni tsukureru menyū o goshōkai shimashō.

And now I'd like to introduce some dishes that are both nutritious and a snap to prepare.

☞ *kisaku (na)* 気さく(な)

An advertising industry favorite, *kigaru ni* is used—somewhat hopefully—to allay the fears of prospective customers who might be reluctant to enter a certain place of business, a mahjong parlor, for example (thinking it might be a hangout for punks and hustlers), or an expensive-looking restaurant (out of concern that they will be stuck with picking up a large tab), or even an optician's. I recently received junk mail from a optician inviting me to "drop by anytime" (*Okigaru ni o tachiyori kudasai*) to have my glasses cleaned or adjusted.

ki ga kawaru　気が変わる　*ki* changes

■ blow hot and cold, change *one's* mind, feel differently about, flip-flop, have a change of heart, think better of

❑ なにしろしょっちゅう気が変わるんだから、こっちはたまったもん
じゃないさ。

Nanishiro shotchū ki ga kawaru n' da kara, kotchi wa tamatta mon ja nai sa.

No way I'm gonna just let it slide the way he's always going and changing his mind every few minutes.

❑ 気が変わりやすい人だから、早くはんこをもらってしまったほうが
勝ちだよ。

Ki ga kawariyasui hito da kara, hayaku hanko o moratte shimatta hō ga kachi da yo.

He's so fickle that you'd be better off getting him to sign on the dotted line as soon as you can.

❑ 出不精のお父さんの気が変わらないうちに家族旅行の計画を立てる
ことにした。

Debushō no otōsan no ki ga kawaranai uchi ni kazoku-ryokō no keikaku o tateru koto ni shita.

My dad's not much for going out, so we started making plans for the family vacation before he had any second thoughts.

❑ 環境が変われば気も変わるだろう。

Kankyō ga kawareba ki mo kawaru darō.

When you're in different surroundings, you'll look at things differently.

☞ *uwakippoi* 浮気っぽい, *uwaki na* 浮気な (both mentioned, though not exemplified, under *uwaki* 浮気)

ki ga kiku 気が利く   *ki* works

1. be considerate, tactful, thoughtful

❑ 彼は若いがなかなか気が利く。

Kare wa wakai ga nakanaka ki ga kiku.

He may be young, but he's really quite considerate. / He's got pretty good judgement for someone his age.

❑ さすがに秘書の経験が長いだけあって気が利く方ですね。

Sasuga ni hisho no keiken ga nagai dake atte ki ga kiku kata desu ne.

It must be all that secretarial experience that has made her so thoughtful.

❑ お茶も出してないのか。まったく気が利かないな。

Ocha mo dashite nai no ka. Mattaku ki ga kikanai na.

Hasn't even served the tea, huh? I don't know where her head is at (What can she be thinking?).

☞ *ki ga tsuku* 気がつく (#2), *ki ga mawaru* 気が回る

2. be bright, on the ball, quick, sharp, smart, witty

❏ あんな気の利かない奴は見たことない。

Anna ki no kikanai yatsu wa mita koto nai.

I've never seen such a numbskull (dimwit, knucklehead, loser).

❏ そういうのを気が利きすぎて間が抜けてるっていうんだ。

Sō iu no o ki ga kikisugite ma ga nukete 'ru tte iu n' da.

That's what you call being too smart for your own good. / That's a case of thinking you've got all the bases covered, only to find you've forgotten the obvious thing.

❏ あんな場では気の利いた冗談の一つも言って上手に逃げろよ。

Anna ba de wa ki no kiita jōdan no hitotsu mo itte jōzu ni nigero yo.

When you get stuck in a situation like that, you've gotta lay something witty on 'em to get out of it. / When something like that happens, you've gotta do some fancy footwork to extricate yourself.

3. chic, cool, just right

❏ この服のデザインはなかなか気が利いているね。

Kono fuku no dezain wa nakanaka ki ga kiite iru ne.

These threads are really a cool design.

❏ 彼の誕生日に何か気の利いた贈り物したいんだけど、何がいいかしら。

Kare no tanjō-bi ni nanika ki no kiita okurimono shitai n' da kedo, nani ga ii kashira.

I'd like to give him the perfect gift for his birthday. I wonder what'd be good.

When modifying a noun as in senses 2 and 3, the idiom appears almost exclusively as *ki no kiita.*

➡ki o kikasu 気を利かす to work *ki*

■ [try to] be thoughtful, considerate; use *one's* head

❏ 少し気を利かすことも覚えなくちゃ、秘書としては失格だね。

Sukoshi ki o kikasu koto mo oboenakucha, hisho toshite wa shikkaku da ne.

You've got to learn to be more thoughtful. As it is, you can't call yourself a secretary.

❏ 気を利かしたつもりが、余計なお節介になってしまった。

Ki o kikashita tsumori ga, yokei na osekkai ni natte shimatta.

Trying to be considerate (helpful) just ended up causing more problems.

❏ 気を利かして若い二人だけにしてあげた。

Ki o kikashite wakai futari dake ni shite ageta.

Realizing that I might be a third wheel, I left the two young folks to themselves.

Unlike *ki ga kiku*, which is most commonly used about others, *ki o kikasu* is used primarily of oneself, indicating a conscious act of will or intention, or when advising others to act a certain way.

also *ki o kikaseru* 気を利かせる

ki ga ki ja nai 気が気じゃない *ki* is not *ki*

■ be beside *oneself* with worry, be worried to death, not be *oneself* (because of worry)

❏ 買ったばかりの株が下がり始めて毎日気が気じゃない。

Katta bakari no kabu ga sagarihajimete mainichi ki ga ki ja nai.

What with that stock I just bought starting to drop, I'm worrying myself sick every day.

❏ あと1分で新幹線が出るっていうのに姿が見えないんだもの、気が 気じゃなかったわよ。

Ato ippun de shinkan-sen ga deru tte iu no ni sugata ga mienai n' da mono, ki ga ki ja nakatta wa yo.

I was pulling my hair out with you nowhere in sight and the bullet train leaving in one minute.

also *ki ga ki de (wa) nai* 気が気で(は)ない

ki ga kuruu 気が狂う *ki* is deranged

■ go crazy, insane, mad, nuts; flip out, lose it, lose *one's* mind

❏ 今日は気の狂う暑さだね。

Kyō wa ki no kuruu atsusa da ne.

It's hot enough today to drive you up the wall.

❏ その母親は気が狂うほど子供に会いたがっている。

Sono haha-oya wa ki ga kuruu hodo kodomo ni aitagatte iru.

She (that mother) wants desperately to see her child.

❏ 彼女はその知らせを聞いて気も狂わんばかりに泣き出した。

Kanojo wa sono shirase o kiite ki mo kuruwan bakari ni nakidashita.

She started bawling like crazy when she heard the news.

Somewhat more formal than *ki ga chigau*, like it *ki ga kuruu* can be used colloquially to mean "mentally ill," although its primary use is metaphoric.

☞ *ki ga chigau* 気が違う, *ki ga fureru* 気がふれる, and *ki ga hen ni naru* 気が変になる

ki ga shizumu 気が沈む *ki* sinks

■ become melancholy, become sad, be saddened, get depressed, down, bummed out

❐ 入院している姪のことを思うと気が沈む。
Nyūin shite iru mei no koto o omou to ki ga shizumu.
My heart sinks every time I think of my niece in the hospital.

❐ 天気が良くないせいか今朝から気が沈んで何もしたくない。
Tenki ga yoku nai sei ka kesa kara ki ga shizunde nani mo shitaku nai.
I don't know if it's the weather or what, but I've been blue since this morning and haven't felt like doing a thing.

Used of a feeling one gets when thinking of something unpleasant in the past or present, and to be distinguished from *ki ga omoi* (see note thereunder).

☞ *ki ga omoi* 気が重い, *ki ga heru* 気が減る, *ki ga meiru* 気が滅入る
☛ *ki ga hareru* 気が晴れる

ki ga shirenai 気が知れない can't understand *someone's ki*

■ be beyond one, be unable to figure out

❐ こんな悪趣味な服を着る人の気が知れないな。
Konna aku-shumi na fuku o kiru hito no ki ga shirenai na.
I just can't understand how someone could be such a fashion criminal.

❐ あんないい娘をふるなんてあいつの気が知れない。
Anna ii ko o furu nante aitsu no ki ga shirenai.
I just can't figure that guy out, dumping a nice girl like her.

❐ 旦那にあんな好き勝手なことさせて、まったく彼女の気が知れないわ。
Danna ni anna suki-katte na koto sasete, mattaku kanojo no ki ga shirenai wa.

It's beyond me why she lets her husband do whatever he wants all the time.

Found preceded by possessive ~ *no* 〜の.

---

ki ga susumanai 気が進まない *ki* doesn't go forward
■ be disinclined, unwilling, reluctant

❐ 悪い話じゃないと思うんだけど、今一つ気が進まないんだ。
Warui hanashi ja nai to omou n' da kedo, ima hitotsu ki ga susumanai n' da.
I don't think it's a particularly bad deal; it's just that I can't get real enthusiastic about it.

❐ あまり気が進まないのなら無理にとは言わない。
Amari ki ga susumanai no nara muri ni to wa iwanai.
If you don't feel like doing it, I'm not going to force you. / If you can't get into doing it, I won't twist your arm.

While the positive form of this idiom can be found, it is all but exclusively seen in dictionaries and seldom, if ever, occurs in speech.

☞ *ki ga noranai* 気が乗らない (see under *ki ga noru* 気が乗る)
☛ *ki ga noru* 気が乗る, *noriki (na)* 乗り気(な) (see under *ki ga noru* 気が乗る)

ki ga sumu 気が済む *ki* is finished
■ be content, satisfied; have enough, have had *one's* fill

❐ 俺が悪かった。気が済むまで殴ってくれ。
Ore ga warukatta. Ki ga sumu made nagutte kure.
It's all my fault. Go ahead, pound on me to your heart's content.

❐ あなたの気が済むようにしてちょうだい。
Anata no ki ga sumu yō ni shite chōdai.
Feel free to do what you want. / Suit yourself.

❐ 言いたいことは全部言って、やっと気が済んだ。
Iitai koto wa zenbu itte, yatto ki ga sunda.
I feel better now that I've finally had my say.

❐ こんなことぐらいじゃまだ気が済まないぜ。
Konna koto gurai ja mada ki ga sumanai ze.
This is hardly enough to satisfy me. / I'm not finished with you yet, man.

ki ga seku 気が急く *ki* hurries

■ be in a hurry, in a rush; champ at the bit

❐ 約束の時間を10分も過ぎているので、気が急く。
Yakusoku no jikan o juppun mo sugite iru no de, ki ga seku.
Ten minutes late already, I've gotta step on it.

❐ 気ばかり急いて一向にはかどらないよ、困ったもんだ。
Ki bakari seite ikkō ni hakadoranai yo, komatta mon da.
I'm running around like a chicken with its head cut off but not making a bit of headway.

   ☞ *ki ga hayaru* 気がはやる (see under *ki ga hayai* 気が早い)
   ⇨ *(ki ga) aseru* (気が)焦る, *kokoro ga hayaru* 心がはやる

ki ga tashika (na) 気が確か(な) certain *ki*

■ be all there, in *one's* right mind, sane, together; have both oars in the water

❐ 年はとっても気は確かだ。
Toshi wa totte mo ki wa tashika da.
I may be getting along in years, but I still know the score (what time it is).

❐ あんな待遇のいい会社をやめるなんて、気が確かとはとても思えない。
Anna taigū no ii kaisha o yameru nante, ki ga tashika to wa totemo omoenai.
You ought to have your head examined, quitting a company that's as good to its employees as yours is.

❐ 彼女に誘われて断った？　気は確かかい？
Kanojo ni sasowarete kotowatta? Ki wa tashika kai?
What are you, one brick short of a load, turning her down when she asked you out?

❐ また金利が下がるらしいが、日銀総裁は気が確かなのか。
Mata kinri ga sagaru rashii ga, Nichi-gin sōsai wa ki ga tashika na no ka.
With interest rates apparently headed down again, I've got to wonder if the governor of the Bank of Japan knows what he's doing.

Appears regularly in rhetorical questions.

   ☞ *shōki* 正気, *ki o tashika ni motsu* 気を確かに持つ (under *ki o ~ motsu* 気を～持つ)

☛ *ki ga chigau* 気が違う, *ki ga hen (na)* 気が変(な) (see under *ki ga hen ni naru* 気が変になる)

ki ga tatsu 気が立つ *ki* stands up

■ be (get) agitated, aroused, flustered, hot, on edge, ruffled, wrought up

❑ 気が立つのはよく分かるが、もっと穏やかに話し合えないものかな。

Ki ga tatsu no wa yoku wakaru ga, motto odayaka ni hanashiaenai mono ka na.

I know it upsets you, but we ought to be able to talk this thing out more calmly.

❑ こちらもつい気が立って失礼なことを言ってしまった。

Kochira mo tsui ki ga tatte shitsurei na koto o itte shimatta.

I got a little excited (on edge) myself and got out of line.

❑ 今は気が立っているから誰が何を言っても無理だと思うよ。

Ima wa ki ga tatte iru kara dare ga nani o itte mo muda da to omou yo.

He's so edgy (worked up) now that I don't think he gives a hoot what anyone says.

Not to be confused with *hara ga tatsu* 腹が立つ, which always means to get angry, *ki ga tatsu* most commonly implies only agitation although it can be used synonymously with *hara ga tatsu*.

⇨ *iradatsu* 苛立つ, *iraira suru* いらいらする

ki ga chiisai 気が小さい *ki* is small

■ feel inhibited; be chickenhearted, fainthearted, lily-livered, meek; be a chicken, a weenie

❑ 田中さんはふだんは気が小さいのに、飲むと人が変わってしまう。

Tanaka-san wa fudan wa ki ga chiisai no ni, nomu to hito ga kawatte shimau.

Tanaka's usually such a wimp, but when he gets a few drinks in him he becomes a different person.

❑ そんなことでくよくよ悩むとは、君も意外と気が小さいんだな。

Sonna koto de kuyokuyo nayamu to wa, kimi mo igai to ki ga chiisai n' da na.

I never figured you for such a weenie that you'd fret over something like that.

☞ *ki ga yowai* 気が弱い
⇨ *shōshin (na)* 小心(な)

ki ga chigau 気が違う *ki* is different

■ go (be) crazy, nuts, out of *one's* mind; be off *one's* rocker

❐ あの日以来気が違ったように勉強している。
Ano hi irai ki ga chigatta yō ni benkyō shite iru.
He's been studying like mad from that day on.

Ki ga chigau is used almost exclusively in its metaphoric sense in the phrase *ki ga chigatta yō ni* or as a rhetorical question in *ki de mo chigatta n' ja nai ka*. The standard expressions for "mentally ill" are *seishin ni ijō o kitasu* 精神に異常を来す or *seishin-byō ni naru* 精神病に なる.

➡kichigai 気違い differing *ki*

■ [a person] a crackpot, loony, lunatic, madman, maniac, nut, psycho, screwball; [a mental state] insanity, madness; [a temporary condition] crazy, insane, nuts, off *one's* rocker, way out there

---

Kichigai and its derivatives (as well as, to a lesser extent, *ki ga kuruu*, *ki ga fureru*, *ki ga hen ni naru*, and *kyōki*) are now considered by many to be political incorrect and highly discriminatory or offensive in almost any situation. Words and phrases that appear innocuous to the non-native can often be sources of ill will. Today both literal and figurative usage of these words is shunned by newspapers and broadcast media, though the latter (figurative meaning) remains common in colloquial speech. Even in figurative form, however, there is a wide range of acceptability according to the degree of metaphorical sense. *Eiga-kichigai* (a movie freak), for example, would likely have the widest range of acceptance and seem free of any negative implications, but even it would be found unacceptable by those who are particularly sensitive to this aspect of language. Thus the student is advised to proceed with utmost caution in this area, and beginning and intermediate students might do best to study the vocabulary here more for comprehension than actual use in speech. In particular, *kichigai* and its derivatives should be avoided when referring to someone with a mental disability, whether in a literal or figurative sense. The examples given in this book are of the type mostly likely to be encountered in conversation among people who possess no special awareness of this aspect of the language.

KI GA CHIRU 49

❏ 私の息子は大学に入るために気違いのようになって（気違いみたいに）勉強しています。

Watshi no musuko wa daigaku ni hairu tame ni kichigai no yō ni natte (kichigai mitai ni) benkyō shite imasu.

My son is studying like crazy in order to get into college.

➡kichigai-zata 気違い沙汰 madness, lunacy

❏ こんな時期に借金で新しく設備投資をするなんて気違い沙汰だ。

Konna jiki ni shakkin de atarashiku setsubi-tōshi o suru nante kichigai-zata da.

It's sheer madness to make capital outlays on borrowed money in this [economic] climate.

➡kichigai-jimiru 気違いじみる to be a little different-*ki*'ed

■ (a little bit) crazy, cracked, nutty

❏ そんな気違いじみたスケジュールで働いたら、からだこわします。

Sonna kichigai-jimita sukejūru de hataraitara, karada kowashimasu.

You're going to ruin your health if you work at an idiotic pace like this.

➡~ kichigai ~ 気違い different-*ki*'ed

■ [preceded by a noun] an addict, a buff, devotee, enthusiast, fan

❏ 若い頃は映画気違いと言われたが、今では有名な映画評論家だ。

Wakai koro wa eiga-kichigai to iwareta ga, ima de wa yūmei na eiga-hyōronka da.

They called him a movie freak when he was young, but look at him now—a famous film critic.

❏ ギャンブル気違いの亭主を持って、彼女も苦労してるに違いないよ。

Gyanburu-kichigai no teishu o motte, kanojo mo kurō shite iru ni chigainai yo.

With that dyed-in-the-wool gambler husband she's strapped with, life can't be easy.

❏ 私は自他ともに認める猫気違いだ。

Watashi wa jita-tomo ni mitomeru neko-kichigai da.

Everyone knows what a nut I am about cats. / Everyone knows how cat-crazy I am.

☞ *ki ga kuruu* 気が狂う, *ki ga fureru* 気が触れる, *ki ga hen ni naru* 気が変になる, *kyōki* 狂気

☛ *ki ga tashika* 気が確か, *shōki* 正気

ki ga chiru 気が散る *ki* is scattered

■ be (get) distracted, break *one's* concentration, lose it

❏ 気が散るから計算中は話しかけないでくださいね。

Ki ga chiru kara keisan-chū wa hanashikakenai de kudasai ne.

Don't talk to me when I'm trying to add stuff up 'cause I'll lose track of where I am (break my concentration).

❑ 気が散って勉強できないからもっとテレビの音小さくしてよ。

Ki ga chitte benkyō dekinai kara motto terebi no oto chiisaku shite yo.

I can't concentrate on studying (keep my mind on my studies) with the TV so loud. Turn it down, would you?

This is what happens to you when your *ki* "gets taken" (*ki o torareru*).

---

ki ga tsuku 気がつく *ki* gets attached

1. be aware of, realize, pick up on, [eventually] come to *one*, dawn on *one*, think of

❑ ふっと気がつくともう40なのよね。

Futto ki ga tsuku to mō yonjū na no yo ne.

I was forty almost before I knew it. / It's like all of a sudden I was forty, you know. / The big four-oh snuck right up on me.

❑ あっちの席の人ずっとあなたのこと見てるわよ。気がついた？

Atchi no seki no hito zutto anata no koto mite 'ru wa yo. Ki ga tsuita?

The guy sitting over there has been eyeing you for quite a while. Did you notice?

❑ 気がついた時にやっとかないと忘れちゃうよ。

Ki ga tsuita toki ni yattokanai (= yatte okanai) to wasurechau yo.

If I don't do it when it comes (occurs) to me, I'll forget all about it.

❑ もういい加減に気がついてもいいはずだけど。

Mō iikagen ni ki ga tsuite mo ii hazu da kedo.

Jeez, it's really about time she woke up and smelled the coffee (saw the light).

❑ 気がつかないふりをしてるに決まってるよ。

Ki ga tsukanai furi o shite 'ru ni kimatte 'ru yo.

I bet he's just pretending like he hasn't noticed.

❑ さっきから手を振っているのにまだ気がついてくれないんだ。

Sakki kara te o futte iru no ni mada ki ga tsuite kurenai n' da.

I've been waving at her for a while now, but she still hasn't seen me.

❑ これは気がつきませんで、失礼しました。

Kore wa ki ga tsukimasen de, shitsurei shimashita.

Sorry I didn't notice you were empty. (said, for example, while pouring someone's beer)

2. attentive, considerate, thoughtful

❑ まだお若いのによく気がつく娘さんですね。

Mada owakai no ni yoku ki ga tsuku musume-san desu ne.

My, what a thoughtful young lady she is!

❑ 細かいことには気のつかない子だけどばりばり仕事を片づけるん だ。

Komakai koto ni wa ki no tsukanai ko da kedo baribari shigoto o katazukeru n' da.

She's not very attentive to detail, but she does pump out the work.

    ☞ *ki ga kiku* 気が利く (meaning #1), *ki ga mawaru* 気が回る

3. regain consciousness, come back to *one's* senses, come to, come around, wake up

❑ もうすぐ麻酔がさめて気がつくはずだ。

Mō sugu masui ga samete ki ga tsuku hazu da.

He should be coming around soon, now that the anesthesia is wearing off.

❑ 気がついたら駅のベンチで寝ていた。

Ki ga tsuitara eki no benchi de nete ita.

When I came to, I was lying on a bench in the station.

    ☛ *ki o ushinau* 気を失う

➡kizuku 気づく attach *ki*

■ be aware of, discover, find out, get wind of, occur to *one*, perceive, sense

❑ そんなことぐらい気づくべきだよ。

Sonna koto gurai kizuku beki da yo.

You have to think of those kinds of things.

❑ 彼が気づくのを待った。

Kare ga kizuku no o matta.

I waited for him to recognize me.

❑ 煙に気づいた時はすでに遅かった。

Kemuri ni kizuita toki wa sude ni osokatta.

It was already too late when I noticed the smoke.

❑ 彼がどんなに大変か、誰も少しも気づかなかった。

Kare ga donna ni taihen ka, dare mo sukoshi mo kizukanakatta.

No one had the slightest inkling of what he was going through.

Generally speaking, *ki ga tsuku* is somewhat more concrete and colloquial whereas *kizuku* is more abstract and literary.

---

ki ga tsumaru 気が詰まる *ki* gets clogged

■ feel ill at ease, uncomfortable, uneasy

❒ あんな堅苦しい気が詰まる会じゃ懇親会にはならないさ。

Anna katakurushii ki ga tsumaru kai ja konshin-kai ni wa naranai sa.

How can they possibly think a formal, stuffy party like that could ever be a "mixer?"

❒ お作法の先生と一緒だもの、気が詰まって食事どころじゃなかったわ。

Osahō no sensei to issho da mono, ki ga tsumatte shokuji dokoro ja nakatta wa.

I was with an etiquette teacher, for heaven's sake! I was so self-conscious there was no way I could have actually eaten anything.

❒ 今日みたいに気の詰まるような思いをしたのは初めてだよ。

Kyō mitai ni ki no tsumaru yō na omoi o shita no wa hajimete da yo.

I've never felt as uncomfortable as I did today.

➡kizumari (na) 気詰まり(な) stuck *ki*

■ awkward, ill at ease, tense, uncomfortable, uptight

❒ 彼女が義理でつきあってくれたのが見え見えで気詰まりだったよ。

Kanojo ga giri de tsukiatte kureta no ga miemie de kizumari datta yo.

It was really awkward for me since it was plain to see that she was just seeing me out of a sense of obligation.

❒ 喧嘩してから仲直りするまでの1週間はなんとも気詰まりな毎日だった。

Kenka shite kara nakanaori suru made no isshū-kan wa nan to mo kizumari na mainichi datta.

I was uptight as could be for the whole week after the argument until we finally made up.

❒ あの人といるとあまり話すことがなくて気詰まりだ。

Ano hito to iru to amari hanasu koto ga nakute kizumari da.

I feel uneasy when I'm around him because we don't have much to talk about.

ki ga tsuyoi 気が強い *ki* is strong

■ determined, hardheaded, headstrong, iron-willed, strong-willed, tenacious, feisty, game, gutsy, plucky, spunky, stubborn, tough, willful, have a mind of *one's* own, stand *one's* ground, put *one's* foot down

❒ 隣の奥さんは見るからに*気が強そうな人だ。

Tonari no okusan wa miru kara ni ki ga tsuyosō na hito da.

You can tell that guy's wife next door is one tough cookie just from the look of her.

* *miru kara ni*: at a glance (it is plain to see); a set phrase.

❑ 彼女は仕事はできるが気が強過ぎて同僚としてはやりにくい。

Kanojo wa shigoto wa dekiru ga ki ga tsuyosugite dōryō toshite wa yari-nikui.

She does her job, but she's just too ornery to work with.

Ki ga tsuyoi describes a character trait, and while it can be either neu-tral or approbatory in the sense of "resolute," it is more often derogato-ry, especially when used about someone the speaker feels should be compliant—a woman or a subordinate in the workplace—and connotes contrariness or intractability. By comparison, *tsuyoki (na)* is neutral and describes an attitude or stance on a particular issue.

also *kizuyoi* 気強い [preceeding a noun]

➡tsuyoki (na) 強気(な) strong *ki*

■ aggressive, firm, hard-nosed, tough; [of the stock market] bullish

❑ ずいぶん強気な発言だな。

Zuibun tsuyoki na hatsugen da na.

You don't mince words, do you. / You seem pretty confident.

❑ いつもながら強気な人だな。

Itsumo-nagara tsuyoki na hito da na.

He's his usual pushy (in-your-face) self.

❑ あの人が相手なら強気に出た方が成功するだろう。

Ano hito ga aite nara tsuyoki ni deta hō ga seikō suru darō.

You'd better play hardball when you're dealing with him. You're more likely to succeed that way.

☛ *yowaki (na)* 弱気(な) (under *ki ga yowai* 気が弱い)

☞ *kachiki (na)* 勝ち気(な), *ki o tsuyoku motsu* 気を強く持つ (see under *ki o ~ motsu* 気を~持つ)

☛ *ki ga yowai* 気が弱い

ki ga tōku naru 気が遠くなる *ki* grows distant

1. black (pass) out, faint, go out like a light, lose con-sciousness, slip into unconsciousness (darkness); feel faint, lightheaded

❑ 君は血を見ると気が遠くなるから、医者にはなれないね。

Kimi wa chi o miru to ki ga tōku naru kara, isha ni wa narenai ne.

You might as well forget ever becoming a doctor, the way you pass out (get dizzy) every time you see blood.

❐ 満員電車に揺られてるうちに気が遠くなった。

Man'in densha ni yurarete 'ru uchi ni ki ga tōku natta.

The train was packed, and I started feeling woozy as it rocked back and forth.

☞ *ki o ushinau* 気を失う, *kizetsu suru* 気絶する (see under *kizetsu*)

2. [of a person] be stupefied; [of something] humongous, dizzying, stupendous

❐ 息子が警察に逮捕されたと聞かされたときは、気が遠くなりそうだった。

Musuko ga keisatsu ni taiho sareta to kikasareta toki wa, ki ga tōku narisō datta.

I was stupefied (flabbergasted) when I was told that my son had been arrested by the police.

❐ あの星の光は、気の遠くなるような長い時間かかって地球へ届いたんだよ。

Ano hoshi no hikari wa, ki no tōku naru yō na nagai jikan kakatte chikyū e todoita n' da yo.

The light from that star took so long to reach the Earth that it makes your head spin to think about it.

❐ 今週中にしなければならない仕事を考えると気が遠くなる。

Konshū-chū ni shinakereba naranai shigoto o kangaeru to ki ga tōku naru.

It blows my mind just to think of all the work I've got to get done this week. / I kinda go blank when I think of everything I've got to take care of this week.

❐ 株の損失は気が遠くなるような額だ。

Kabu no sonshitsu wa ki ga tōku naru yō na gaku da.

My stock losses are staggering (mind-boggling).

Although the expression literally means to faint or lose consciousness (*ki o ushinau* 気を失う), it is widely used in a metaphoric sense in conjunction with ~ *narisō da* or ~ *naru yō na* to express shock, amazement, or astonishment at some vast quantity.

---

ki ga togameru 気がとがめる *ki* blames (itself)

■ be conscience-stricken, repentant; blame *oneself*; feel a pang of conscience, guilty, sorry, remorseful; regret

❐ あのときひどいこと言ってしまって、今でも気がとがめる。

Ano toki hidoi koto itte shimatte, ima de mo ki ga togameru.

Some of the terrible things I said then still bother me. / I still feel bad about some of the horrible things I said then.

❐ 気がとがめて彼の顔がまともに見られなかった。

Ki ga togamete kare no kao ga matomo ni mirarenakatta.

I felt so guilty I couldn't even look him square in the eye.

❐ 人を裏切ってちっとも気がとがめない奴の気が知れないなあ。

Hito o uragitte chittomo ki ga togamenai yatsu no ki ga shirenai nā.

I just can't understand how somebody could think nothing of double-crossing a friend like that.

❐ 自分が悪いことをしたとは思わないから、全然気がとがめない。

Jibun ga warui koto o shita to wa omowanai kara, zenzen ki ga togamenai.

I'm not a bit sorry, 'cause I don't feel I did anything wrong.

  ⇨ *ki ga sasu* 気が差す

ki ga nai 気がない no *ki*

■ feel blah, be lackadaisical, be listless; be uninterested (in), not be interested (in), have no taste for, not like

❐ 気がないのなら早くそう言ってあげた方が彼女のためだよ。

Ki ga nai no nara hayaku sō itte ageta hō ga kanojo no tame da yo.

If you don't feel anything for her, the sooner you tell her the better off she'll be.

❐ もったいぶって*気がない素振りなんかしてると彼に逃げられちゃうわよ。

Mottai-butte ki ga nai soburi nanka shite 'ru to kare ni nigerarechau wa yo.

If you keep playing it cool like you're not interested in him, he's going to find himself someone else.

  * *mottai-buru*: lit., act no thing; to put on airs (when there is no justification)

❐ なんだか気のない返事だね。

Nan da ka ki no nai henji da ne.

That's a half-assed (lukewarm) answer if I've ever heard one.

Not to be confused with ~ *ki ga nai*, which is found under *ki*.

☛ *ki ga aru* 気がある

ki ga nagai 気が長い *ki* is long

1. [of a person] patient, laid-back, have a long fuse

❒ 彼は気が長いから何ヵ月でも待ってくれると思うよ。

Kare wa ki ga nagai kara nankagetsu de mo matte kureru to omou yo.

He's a patient guy. I imagine he'll wait months for you if he has to.

❒ 大陸の国民は島国の国民より気が長いようだ。

Tairiku no kokumin wa shimaguni no kokumin yori ki ga nagai yō da.

People living on continents seem to have a lot more patience than islanders.

2. [of events and processes] a slow business, take a lot of patience

❒ 百年前に造り始めたこの教会は完成までにもう百年かかるそうだが、気が長い話だね。

Hyakunen-mae ni tsukurihajimeta kono kyōkai wa kansei made ni mō hyakunen kakaru sō da ga, ki ga nagai hanashi da ne.

Imagine it taking another hundred years to finish this church that was started a hundred years ago! They're really in it for the long haul!

❒ そんなに気の長いこと言ってると彼女他の人と結婚しちゃうよ。

Sonna ni ki no nagai koto itte 'ru to kanojo hoka no hito to kekkon shichau yo.

She's gonna up and marry some other guy if you keep drawing things out.

   ☞ *ki ga mijikai* 気が短い

   ⇨ *nonbiri shita* のんびりした

➡kinaga (ni) 気長(に) long *ki*

■ patient(ly), long-suffering; persistent(ly), enduring(ly)

❒ まだ若いんですから気長に見守ってあげましょうよ。

Mada wakai n' desu kara kinaga ni mimamotte agemashō yo.

He's still young, so let's give him a chance. / He's still young, so let's not jump to conclusions about him.

❒ そんなに結果を急がないでもっと気長に考えなさい。

Sonna ni kekka o isoganai de motto kinaga ni kangaenasai.

Don't be in such a hurry to get results. Put a little more thought into it. / Keep your shirt on, and give it some more thought.

   ☞ *ki o nagaku motsu* 気を長く持つ (see under *ki o ~ motsu* 気を~持つ)

ki ga nukeru 気が抜ける *ki* slips out

1. be (feel) disappointed, let down, bummed out; lose heart

❑ そんなこと言わないでよ。こっちまで気が抜けるじゃないか。

Sonna koto iwanai de yo. Kotchi made ki ga nukeru ja nai ka.

Cut it out. Whaddya want to do, bum me out too?

❑ 張り切っていたのに雨で試合が中止になって、気が抜けた。

Harikitte ita no ni ame de shiai ga chūshi ni natte, ki ga nuketa.

I was really up for the game, so it was a big letdown when it got rained out.

❑ 日本チームが代表になれなかったので、サッカーファンもすっかり気が抜けてしまった。

Nihon-chīmu ga daihyō ni narenakatta no de, sakkāfan mo sukkari ki ga nukete shimatta.

Japanese soccer fans were down in the dumps when the national team failed to make the cut.

❑ 経営者側からの回答は気が抜けるような内容だった。

Keieisha-gawa kara no kaitō wa ki ga nukeru yō na naiyō datta.

The response from management was a big disappointment (disappointing / disheartening).

2. go (be) flat, stale; lose (all the) fizz

❑ 気が抜けるとまずいから早く飲んでしまおう。

Ki ga nukeru to mazui kara hayaku nonde shimaō.

We'd better drink up 'cause it's no good once it goes flat.

気の抜けたビールも料理に使えるから捨てなくてもいいよ。

Ki no nuketa bīru mo ryōri ni tsukaeru kara sutenakute mo ii yo.

You can use stale beer to cook with so you don't have to throw it away.

➤ 気が抜けた風船みたいにしょんぼりしている。

Ki ga nuketa fūsen mitai ni shonbori shite iru.

He sure looks deflated (like somebody took the wind out of his sails). [From another meaning of *ki ga nukeru* not included here, "to be punctured or lose air."]

➡ki o nuku 気を抜く take *ki* out

■ let up, relax, become (get) careless, goof off

❑ 気を抜くと、思わぬところで失敗するよ。

Ki o nuku to, omowanu tokoro de shippai suru yo.

Start daydreaming and you'll screw up when you least expect to.

❑ リハーサルはうまくいったのでつい気を抜いたのがよくなかった。

Rihāsaru wa umaku itta no de tsui ki o nuita no ga yoku nakatta.

The rehearsal went so well that I sort of relaxed, and that was a mistake.

❑ 最後まで気を抜かないできちんとやりなさい。

Saigo made ki o nukanai de kichin to yarinasai.

No sloughing off. Don't let up till you've finished everything.

Distinguished from its cognate *ki ga nukeru* insofar as it indicates intentionality or willfulness.

☞ *ki o yurumeru* 気を緩める (see under *ki ga yurumu* 気が緩む)

kigane 気兼ね pile up *ki*

■ uneasiness, discomfort (after taking into account how someone else feels and modifying one's behavior accordingly)

❑ 僕はなぜかあの人には気兼ねがあって、率直にものが言えないんだ。

Boku wa naze ka ano hito ni wa kigane ga atte, sotchoku ni mono ga ienai n' da.

There's something about that guy that keeps me from saying what I think when I'm around him.

❑ どうぞ気兼ねなく分からないことは何でも聞いて下さい。

Dōzo kigane naku wakaranai koto wa nan de mo kiite kudasai.

Please feel free to ask about anything you don't understand.

    ☞ *kizukai* 気遣い (see under *kizukau* 気遣う)

    ⇨ *enryo* 遠慮

    ☛ *kiyasui* 気安い

➡kigane (o) suru 気兼ね(を)する

■ feel (somehow) constrained, uneasy, uncomfortable

❑ 彼女はそんなに気兼ねする性質には見えないが、意外だね。

Kanojo wa sonna ni kigane suru tachi ni wa mienai ga, igai da ne.

She sure doesn't look the type to be ill at ease around people, but you never know, I guess.

❑ 周りの人に気兼ねをして、かわいそうなぐらい小さくなっている。

Mawari no hito ni kigane o shite, kawaisō na gurai chiisaku natte iru.

He's so intimidated by the people around him it's almost sad. / He's so self-conscious that it's almost pathetic.

    ☞ *ki o tsukau* 気を使う

ki ga noru 気が乗る *ki* mounts up

■ get enthusiastic, get going, get into, get turned on (to), get all hopped up (about)

❑ 気が乗ると一晩中でもワープロに向かって仕事をする。

Ki ga noru to hitoban-jū de mo wāpuro ni mukatte shigoto o suru.

I'll pound away on the word processor all night long when I'm on a roll.

❏ あいつ気が乗ったら平気で徹夜もするぜ。

Aitsu ki ga nottara heiki de tetsuya mo suru ze.

Hey, when he gets all pumped up about something, he'll stay up all night, no sweat.

❏ 今度の計画にはあまり気が乗らない。

Kondo no keikaku ni wa amari ki ga noranai.

I'm not too hot on (can't get too worked up about) the project.

❏ 社内旅行は申し込みはしたが何となく気が乗らない。

Shanai-ryokō wa mōshikomi wa shita ga nan to naku ki ga noranai.

I applied to go along on the company trip this time, but for some reason I just can't seem to get excited about it.

❏ 一応こちらの話は聞いてくれたんですが、あまり気が乗らない様子でした。

Ichiō kochira no hanashi wa kiite kureta n' desu ga, amari ki ga noranai yōsu deshita.

They listened to what I had to say, but they didn't show much interest.

The idiom is most often encountered in the negative.

☛ *ki ga susumanai* 気が進まない

➡ kinori (ga) suru 気乗り(が)する get *ki* mounted
■ an interest (in), an inclination (to do); a notion (to do)

❏ あまり気乗りするアイデアじゃないが背に腹はかえられない*。

Amari kinori suru aidea ja nai ga se ni hara wa kaerarenai.

It's not exactly one of my favorite ideas, but I suppose we'll just have to bite the bullet on this one.

 * *se ni hara wa kaerarenai:* lit., can't change one's stomach into one's back; to be unavoidable, no way out.

❏ 先生は熱心に進めてくれる会社だが、どうも気乗りがしない。

Sensei wa nesshin ni susumete kureru kaisha da ga, dōmo kinori ga shinai.

My teacher is really pushing (enthusiastically recommending) this company [as a place of work], but there's something about it that turns me off.

➡ kinori-usu (na) 気乗り薄(な) weak-mounted *ki* lukewarm, unenthusiastic, halfhearted

❏ 大暴落以来、一般投資家は優良株にも気乗り薄だ。

Dai-bōraku irai, ippan tōshi-ka wa yūryō-kabu ni mo kinori-usu da.

Ever since the market crashed, private investors have even been shying away from the blue chips.

❏ 気乗り薄な返事だったから、もう一度当たってみます。

Kinori-usu na henji datta kara, mō ichido atatte mimasu.
Their reply was pretty lukewarm, so I'll try them again.

Appears most commonly in the negative.

➡noriki (na) 乗り気(な) mounted *ki*

■ eagerness, enthusiasm (for)

❏ 先方は乗り気ですから、気が変わらないうちに契約してしまいましょう。

Senpō wa noriki desu kara, ki ga kawaranai uchi ni keiyaku shite shimaimashō.

The other party's interested, so let's get the contract signed before they change their minds.

❏ 僕は乗り気だったんだが、女房がどうしてもいやだと言い張ってね。

Boku wa noriki datta n' da ga, nyōbō ga dōshite mo iya da to iihatte ne.

I was all ready to go ahead with it, but the wife wouldn't hear of it. / I thought it sounded great, but the better half wouldn't have anything to do with it.

❏ 今度の話にはずいぶん乗り気になっているようですね。

Kondo no hanashi ni wa zuibun noriki ni natte iru yō desu ne.

You really seem to be high on (up for) the project this time.

❏ せっかく乗り気になっていたら、向こうから断わられてしまった。

Sekkaku noriki ni natte itara, mukō kara kotowararete shimatta.

They pulled the plug [on the project] just when I was getting into it.

❏ 三時間ぐらいねばって説明したら、やっと乗り気になってくれましたよ。

Sanji-kan gurai nebatte setsumei shitara, yatto noriki ni natte kuremashita.

They finally showed some interest after I explained things for about three hours. / It took around three hours of explaining, but they finally came around (warmed up to it).

❏ ぜんぜん乗り気じゃなかったから、断られてむしろ幸いだった。

Zenzen noriki ja nakatta kara, kotowararete mushiro saiwai datta.

I wasn't into it at all, so I was actually glad when it fell through.

☞ *ki ga muku* 気が向く

ki ga hairu 気が入る *ki* comes in

■ get into *doing something*, be enthusiastic *about something*, put *one's* mind to *doing something*

❒ 気が入ると実にいい絵を描く人だ。

Ki ga hairu to jitsu ni ii e o kaku hito da.

He can really paint when he puts his mind to it (gets into it).

❒ ずいぶん気の入った仕事ぶりだ。

Zuibun ki no haitta shigoto buri da.

She's really into her work.

Compared to *ki o ireru*, *ki ga hairu* implies that there is less effort or intentionality involved.

☞ *ki o ireru* 気を入れる

ki ga hazumu 気が弾む *ki* bounces

■ become buoyant, get excited, be in high spirits

❒ 春のイタリア旅行のことを考えると気が弾むよ。

Haru no Itaria ryokō no koto o kangaeru to ki ga hazumu yo.

I get excited (hyped) just thinking about our trip to Italy in the spring.

気が弾んで、つい鼻歌が出ちゃった。

Ki ga hazunde, tsui hanauta ga dechatta.

I was so high that I found myself humming a little tune.

⇨ *kokoro ga hazumu* 心が弾む

ki ga hayai 気が早い *ki* is fast

■ be hasty, impatient; get ahead of *oneself*

❒ まだ恋人もいないのにもう結婚式場を予約したなんて、ずいぶん気
が早いね。

*Mada koibito mo inai no ni mō kekkon-shikijō o yoyaku shita nante,
zuibun ki ga hayai ne.*

Don't you think you're jumping the gun a little, reserving a wedding
chapel when you haven't even got a girlfriend?

❒ 気の早い吉田さんは、生まれたばかりの息子の大学進学の心配をし
ている。

*Ki no hayai Yoshida-san wa, umareta bakari no musuko no daigaku-
shingaku no shinpai o shite iru.*

That Yoshida's so far ahead of himself that he's already worrying about
his newborn son getting into college.

⇨ *sekkachi (na)* せっかち(な)

➡ki ga hayaru 気がはやる *ki* hurries

■ be hasty, impatient, impetuous, rash

❒ 気がはやって新記録が出せなかった。

Ki ga hayatte shin-kiroku ga dasenakatta.

I tried too hard and was unable to set a new record.

❒ 落ち着いてよ。気がはやるとうまくいかないからさ。

Ochitsuite yo. Ki ga hayaru to umaku ikanai kara sa.

Take it easy! You'll screw everything up if you get impatient.

   ☞ *ki ga seku* 気が急く

   ⇨ *(ki ga) aseru* (気が)焦る, *kokoro ga hayaru* 心がはやる

ki ga haru 気が張る *ki* is stretched out

■ be anxious, strung-out, tense, under stress, uptight; [〜の〜] stressful, nerve-racking

❒ 今日見えるのは気難しい人ばかりだからほんとうに気が張るわ。

Kyō mieru no wa kimuzukashii hito bakari da kara hontō ni ki ga haru wa.

I'm uptight because I'm meeting a bunch of really difficult people today. / The people I'm supposed to see today are all difficult to please, so I'm kind of anxious about it.

❒ 気の張る集まりじゃありませんから、ぜひ一度どうぞ。

Ki no haru atsumari ja arimasen kara, zehi ichido dōzo.

You ought to try to make it to one of our little get-togethers. They're not pretentious at all.

❒ 今はまだ気が張っているから元気そうだが、一段落してからが心配だ。

Ima wa mada ki ga hatte iru kara genkisō da ga, ichi-danraku shite kara ga shinpai da.

She seems lively enough now while she's still keyed up, but I'm worried what'll happen when things settle down a bit.

ki ga hareru 気が晴れる *ki* clears up

■ feel better, relieved, lighthearted, like a weight has been lifted from *one's* shoulders

❒ このあいだからひっかかっていたことが解決して、やっと気が晴れた。

Kono aida kara hikkakatte ita koto ga kaiketsu shite, yatto ki ga hareta.

That stuff I'd had on my mind finally got worked out, so I feel like it's clear sailing from here on out.

❒ 亭主と喧嘩してむしゃくしゃしてたんだけど、パチンコしたら気が晴れちゃった。

Teishu to kenka shite mushakusha shite 'ta n' da kedo, pachinko shitara ki ga harechatta.

I got all worked up fighting with my old man, but felt a whole lot better after playing pachinko for a while.

Unlike *ki ga raku ni naru* 気が楽になる, which expresses only a freedom from concern or worry, and *ki ga karuku naru* 気が軽くなる, which signals the relief arising from completion of some duty (usually a job), *ki ga hareru* can also express a return to calm once anger has subsided.

☞ *ki ga shizumu* 気が沈む

➡ki o harasu 気を晴らす clear up *one's ki*

■ divert *oneself*, do *something* to take *one's* mind off *one's* problems, [do *something* to] forget *one's* troubles

❐ 気を晴らすのに何かいい方法はないだろうか。

Ki o harasu no ni nanika ii hōhō wa nai darō ka.

You don't know a good way I can get my mind off my troubles, do you?

❐ 少し外へ出て気を晴らさないとこのままでは病気になってしまうよ。

Sukoshi soto e dete ki o harasanai to kono mama de wa byōki ni natte shimau yo.

If you don't get out to clear the air, you'll end up making yourself sick.

➡kibarashi 気晴(ら)し *ki* clearing

■ a change of pace, (for) a change, diversion, relaxation

❐ 家にばかり閉じこもっていないで、たまには気晴らしをしに出かけなさい。

Uchi ni bakari tojikomotte inai de, tama ni wa kibarashi o shi ni dekake-nasai.

Don't just shut yourself up in the house all the time; get out and do something for a change.

❐ 気晴らしに駅前のパチンコ屋へちょっと行ってくるよ。

Kibarashi ni ekimae no pachinko-ya e chotto itte kuru yo.

I'm going to the pachinko parlor in front of the station for a while to relax (to calm my nerves, veg out).

ki ga hikishimaru 気が引き締まる *ki* tightens

■ be determined (resolved) to do *something*

❐ 正装すると気が引き締まるものだね。

Seisō suru to ki ga hikishimaru mono da ne.

There's something about getting dressed up that makes you feel like a new person.

❐ 辞令をもらって、気が引き締まる思いがした。

Jirei o moratte, ki ga hikishimaru omoi ga shita.

I had pause to reflect on things when I received my official notice of appointment.

⇨ *kokoro ga hikishimaru* 心が引き締まる

➥ki o hikishimeru 気を引き締める tighten *ki*

■ get *oneself* worked up for, screw *oneself* up for (to do) *something*, steel *oneself*

❐ 気を引き締めるために当分酒を断とうと思う。

Ki o hikishimeru tame ni tōbun sake o tatō to omou.

I'm going to lay off the booze for a while and get my act together.

❐ 中日まで全勝の貴錦はいっそう気を引き締めていた。

Nakabi made zenshō no Takanishiki wa issō ki o hikishimete ita.

With a perfect 8-0 going into the ninth day of the tournament, [the Sumo wrestler] Takanishiki was really psyched up.

❐ チーム全員が気を引き締めて決勝戦に臨んでもらいたい。

Chīmu zen'in ga ki o hikishimete kesshō-sen ni nozonde moraitai.

I want everybody on the team to pull himself together and get focused on the championship.

❐ 油断大敵だ。気を引き締めてかかれ。

Yudan-taiteki da. Ki o hikishimete kakare.

Letting up now is the worst thing you can do. You've gotta want it. Now go out there and give 'em hell!

ki ga hikeru 気が引ける *ki* pulls in

■ feel funny, diffident, timid, timorous, can't get into

❐ こんな恰好だから入るの気が引けるよ。

Konna kakkō da kara hairu no ki ga hikeru yo.

It just doesn't feel right going in dressed like this.

❐ 彼の誘いを断ってこのまま帰るのは少し気が引ける。

Kare no sasoi o kotowatte kono mama kaeru no wa sukoshi ki ga hikeru.

I can't very well simply leave after turning him down the way I did.

❐ まわりの人がそうそうたるメンバーだったので、気が引けて何も発言できなかった。

Mawari no hito ga sōsō-taru menbā datta no de, ki ga hikete nani mo hatsugen dekinakatta.

With all the heavyweights there, I couldn't bring myself to speak up.

KI GA FUSAGU 65

ki ga fusagu 気がふさぐ *ki* closes up

■ be blue, be in low spirits, be low, get depressed

❐ この地方の冬は曇の日ばかりで実に気がふさぐね。

Kono chihō no fuyu wa kumori no hi bakari de jitsu ni ki ga fusagu ne.

The way it's overcast every day during the winter in this region can really get depressing.

❐ わけもなく気がふさいで、何をするのも嫌なんです。

Wake mo naku ki ga fusaide, nani o suru no mo iya nan desu.

I'm just moping around all the time and can't get into doing anything at all.

Commonly heard in conversation with *ki* omitted and no change in meaning. See the examples below.

➤ 最近ひどくふさいでるじゃないか、お前。

Saikin hidoku fusaide 'ru ja nai ka, omae.

You've really been bummed out lately, haven't ya? / You've sure been draggin' ass lately.

➤ ふさいだ顔していったいどうしちゃったの。

Fusaida kao shite ittai dō shichatta no.

What's the long face all about? / How come you're so down in the mouth?

ki ga fureru 気がふれる *ki* is touched

■ be touched, unbalanced, be out of *one's* mind

❐ 戦争中は気がふれるほど辛い経験をしました。

Sensō-chū wa ki ga fureru hodo tsurai keiken o shimashita.

During the war I experienced some things so terrible that I feared for my sanity.

❐ そんなにいくつも難問をかかえて、気がふれない方が不思議だ。

Sonna ni ikutsu mo nanmon o kakaete, ki ga furenai hō ga fushigi da.

With all the problems you have, it's a wonder that you are able to maintain a balanced outlook.

Literary.

☞ *ki ga chigau* 気が違う, *ki ga kuruu* 気が狂う, *ki ga hen ni naru* 気が変になる

ki ga heru 気が減る *ki* diminishes

■ be depressed, down, worn down

❐ 毎月のように預金金利が下がるので気が減るよ。
Maitsuki no yō ni yokin-kinri ga sagaru no de ki ga heru yo.
It's such a bummer to sit and watch interest rates on savings accounts head south almost every month.

❐ この不景気で注文が少なくなって気が減る思いだ。
Kono fu-keiki de chūmon ga sukunaku natte ki ga heru omoi da.
It's depressing the way orders keep declining during the recession.

❐ 彼の節約ぶりには見ている方が気が減る。
Kare no setsuyaku-buri ni wa mite iru hō ga ki ga heru.
He's so frugal that it's almost pathetic.

Similar to *ki ga meiru* 気が滅入る, *gakkari suru* がっかりする and *genki ga naku naru* 元気がなくなるinsofar as it expresses a sense of depression, the source of that depression is primarily material or financial loss or penury in the case of *ki ga heru*. There is, by the way, no *ki ga hette iru* (present progressive tense), as the idiom describes a condition rather than the process of falling into such a condition.

☞ *ki ga shizumu* 気が沈む, *ki ga meiru* 気が滅入る

ki ga hen ni naru 気が変になる *ki* becomes strange

■ go crazy, nuts; flip out, lose it, lose *one's* marbles

❐ 忙しくて忙しくて、もう気が変になりそうだ。
Isogashikute isogashikute, mō ki ga hen ni narisō da.
I'm so busy I feel like I'm gonna go nuts.

❐ どうして東京の人はこんな満員電車に毎日乗って気が変にならないんだろう。
Dōshite Tōkyō no hito wa konna man'in densha ni mainichi notte ki ga hen ni naranai n' darō.
I wonder how Tokyoites keep from flipping out riding these crowded trains every day.

As with *ki ga chigau*, used primarily in a metaphoric sense.

☞ *ki ga chigau* 気が違う, *ki ga kuruu* 気が狂う, *ki ga fureru* 気が触れる

➥ki ga hen (na) 気が変(な) strange *ki*

■ bonkers, cracked, crazy, have a screw loose, have lost *one's* marbles, insane, mad, off *one's* rocker

❒ あんた気が変なんじゃないの、そんな夢みたいなことばかり言っての。

Anta ki ga hen nan ja nai no, sonna yume mitai na koto bakari itte.

Don't you think you're going off the deed end, always talking about your pie-in-the sky dreams?

❒ このがらくたに100万円も払ったなんて、気が変なのか。

Kono garakuta ni hyakuman-en mo haratta nante, ki ga hen na no ka.

You paid a million yen for a piece of junk like this! Are you out of your mind?

Note that the meaning of this phrase is not synonymous with *hen na ki ga suru* 変な気がする (to feel funny about *something*) and *hen na ki ni naru* 変な気になる (to feel an sudden urge *toward the opposite sex* or to feel a unexpected temptation *to pilfer or steal*).

kigamae 気構え the build of *one's ki*

■ anticipation, preparedness, readiness

❒ 彼の場合、普通の学生とは気構えが違う。

Kare no bāi, futsū no gakusei to wa kigamae ga chigau.

He's different from other students in the way he approaches things.

❒ しっかりした目的意識と気構えがなければ、成功しないよ。

Shikkari shita mokuteki-ishiki to kigamae ga nakereba, seikō shinai yo.

You'll never make a go of it unless you've got a clear goal in mind and you're prepared to see things through.

❒ お互いに一歩もゆずらない気構えだった。

Otagai ni ippo mo yuzuranai kigamae datta.

They both had their heels dug in and weren't about to budge an inch.

⇨ *kokorogamae* 心構え

ki ga magireru 気が紛れる *ki* is diverted

■ be diverted, forget (*one's* worries)

❒ 皆と一緒にいる時は気が紛れるが、一人になるととても淋しい。

Minna to issho ni iru toki wa ki ga magireru ga, hitori ni naru to totemo sabishii.

Being out with friends is a great distraction, but boy do I get lonely when I'm by myself.

❐ 滝本さんからの電話のおかげで気が紛れた。

Takimoto-san kara no denwa no okage de ki ga magireta.

Thanks to Takimoto's call, I forgot all my worries (for a while).

➡ki o magirawasu 気を紛らわす divert *ki*

■ divert *one's* attention, find a diversion, get (take) *one's* mind off

❐ 僕たちが心配しなくても、彼には気を紛らわす方法はたくさんあるさ。

Boku-tachi ga shinpai shinakute mo, kare ni wa ki o magirawasu hōhō wa takusan aru sa.

There's nothing for us to worry about 'cause there are plenty of things he can do to take his mind off his problems.

❐ 昼間はパチンコしたり映画に行ったりして適当に気を紛らわしている。

Hiruma wa pachinko shitari eiga ni ittari shite tekitō ni ki o magirawashite iru.

I'm doing what I can to keep my mind off my problems by playing pinball and going to the movies during the day.

Not to be confused with the related expression *kimagure na* 気紛れ(な), which means "capricious," "fickle" or "whimsical," *ki o magirawasu* indicates intention to escape from an unpleasant emotional state, and in this respect also differs slightly from its cognate *ki ga magireru*, which, although used to describe the same phenomenon, does so by depicting the resulting relief as a natural course of events rather than one specifically sought after or willed.

---

also *ki o magirawaseru* 気を紛らわせる

ki ga mawaru 気が回る *ki* goes around

■ be thoughtful, considerate; be full of (good) ideas

❐ おじょうちゃんはまだ小さいのにずいぶん気が回るのね。

Ojōchan wa mada chiisai no ni zuibun ki ga mawaru no ne.

For such a little girl, you sure are thoughtful.

❐ 忙しかったからそこまで気が回らなかった。

Isogashikatta kara soko made ki ga mawaranakatta.

I was so busy I didn't even think of doing that.

❐ そこまで気が回らないよ。

Soko made ki ga mawaranai yo.

Hey, I can't think of everything, you know.

Not to be confused with its cognate *ki o mawasu* 気を回す, which means to be suspicious and is used critically of others.

☞ *ki ga kiku* 気が利く(#1), *ki ga tsuku* 気がつく (#2)

ki ga mijikai   気が短い   *ki* is short

1. be hotheaded, hot-tempered, quick-tempered, short-tempered, touchy, volcanic; have a short fuse

❐ 家の親父は気が短くてすぐ怒鳴るから、話の切り出し方が難しい。

Uchi no oyaji wa ki ga mijikakute sugu donaru kara, hanashi no kiri-dashi-kata ga muzukashii.

The way my dad's always flying off the handle, it's not easy to bring up the subject.

❐ 結婚するまで夫があんなに気の短い人とは思わなかった。

Kekkon suru made otto ga anna ni ki no mijikai hito to wa omowa-nakatta.

I had no idea my husband had such a short fuse until after we were married.

2. antsy, hasty, impatient, rash, restless

❐ 気が短い人はエレベーターに乗るとすぐ「閉」のボタンを押す。

Ki ga mijikai hito wa erebētā ni noru to sugu "hei" no botan o osu.

Impatient people push the "close" button as soon as they get in an elevator.

❐ そんな気の短いこと言わないで、もう少し時間をくれないか。

Sonna ki no mijikai koto iwanai de, mō sukoshi jikan o kurenai ka.

Think you could back off a bit and give me just a little more time?

 ☞ *ki ga hayai* 気が早い

 ⇨ *sekkachi na* せっかち(な)

tanki   短気   a short *ki*

■ a quick temper, short temper, a short fuse; [~ *o okosu*] get angry (mad), explode, blow up

❐ ここで短気を起こしたら今までの苦労が水の泡*じゃないか。

Koko de tanki o okoshitara ima made no kurō ga mizu no awa ja nai ka.

Blow a fuse now and everything you've worked so hard for will go up in smoke.

 * *mizu no awa*: lit., water bubbles; from the sense of "short/ephemeral" comes, by extension, "useless, wasted"

➡tanki wa sonki 短気は損気 a short *ki* is a losing *ki*

■ impatience can be expensive; a short temper is costly

❐ 「短気は損気」と思って我慢してきたけど、もう嫌だ。

"Tanki wa sonki" to omotte gaman shite kita kedo, mō iya da.

I've told myself all along that getting pissed off would only cost me in the end, but now I've had it up to here.

❐ ここはぐっと我慢しなさい。「短気は損気」だよ。

Koko wa gutto gaman shinasai. "Tanki wa sonki" da yo.

Now's the time you've got to stand there and take it. Get impatient now and it'll cost you. / Hang in there (Tough it out). Fly off the handle now and you'll regret it later.

❐ 「短気は損気」と言うだろう。言い過ぎたら取り返しがつかないよ。

"Tanki wa sonki" to iu darō. Iisugitara torikaeshi ga tsukanai yo.

You know what they say about losing your temper and being sorry later. Go too far now, and you'll never be able to take it back.

Used exclusively to admonish someone about the dangers of losing his temper or growing impatient. *Sonki* is a term created solely to rhyme with *tanki*, and is not seen outside this aphorism.

➡tanki wa tanmei 短気は短命 a short *ki* is a short life

■ a short temper shortens life

❐ カッカしてる親父に「『短気は短命』だよ」と言ったら、ますます怒った。

Kakka shite 'ru oyaji ni "'Tanki wa tanmei' da yo" to ittara, masumasu okotta.

When I told my dad, "That temper of yours will be the death of you," he just got madder.

Used to encourage patience in someone or advise them not to get angry.

➡tanki wa miren no moto 短気は未練の元 a short *ki* is a source of regret

■ get mad and you'll live to regret it

❐ 「短気は未練の元」って知らない？　後悔するかもよ。

"Tanki wa miren no moto" tte shiranai? Kōkai suru kamo yo.

You've heard the axiom "anger causes regret," right? Well, you might be sorry later on [if you lose your temper now].

Similar in meaning and usage to *tanki wa sonki*.

➡tanki (na) 短気(な) short *ki*

■ explosive, short-tempered, have a short fuse

❑ 津山は短気な男だが機嫌を直すのも早いよ。

Tsuyama wa tanki na otoko da ga kigen o naosu no mo hayai yo.

Tsuyama's pretty short-tempered, but he cools down fast, too.

❑ 彼はいいやつだが短気で怒りっぽいのがたまにきずだ。

Kare wa ii yatsu da ga tanki de okorippoi no ga tama ni kizu da.

He's a good enough guy, but that short temper he's got is his one fault.

❑ 家の子は誰に似てあんなに短気なんだろう。

Uchi no ko wa dare ni nite anna ni tanki nan darō.

Sometimes I wonder where that son of mine got such a short temper.

also *kimijika (na)* 気短(な)

⇨ *okorippoi* 怒りっぽい

ki ga muku 気が向く *ki* moves toward

■ be (feel) inclined *to do*, be in the mood *to do*, feel like *doing*

❑ 気が向くと頑張るけど、長続きしないんだよねえ。

Ki ga muku to ganbaru kedo, nagatsuzuki shinai n' da yo nē.

He works hard when he has a mind to, but he never sticks to anything for long.

❑ 気が向いたときにいつでもいらしてください。

Ki ga muita toki ni itsu de mo irashite kudasai.

Come visit any time you take a notion to.

❑ 誘われていることはいるんだが、どうも気が向かないよ。

Sasowarete iru koto wa iru n' da ga, dōmo ki ga mukanai yo.

I've been invited all right, but I just can't get motivated to go.

❑ 足の向くまま気の向くままに世界中を旅してみたいものだ。

Ashi no muku mama ki no muku mama ni sekai-jū o tabi shite mitai mono da.

I'd love to be able to travel around the world wherever my fancy took me.

☞ *noriki ni naru* 乗り気になる, *kinori suru* 気乗りする (see under *ki ga noru* 気が乗る)

ki ga meiru 気が滅入る *ki* is downcast

■ be depressed, bummed out, down; *one's* heart sinks

❏ 雨の日は気が滅入る。

Ame no hi wa ki ga meiru.

Rainy days get me down. / I get bummed out on rainy days.

❏ これ以上気が滅入る話は聞きたくない。

Kore ijō ki ga meiru hanashi wa kikitaku nai.

Enough of all these depressing stories.

❏ そんなこと言わないでよ。そうじゃなくても気が滅入ってるんだから。

Sonna koto iwanai de yo. Sō ja nakute mo ki ga meitte 'ru n' da kara.

Come on, don't give me that! I'm depressed enough as it is.

❏ 君の話を聞いているうちにだんだん気が滅入ってきたよ。

Kimi no hanashi o kiite iru uchi ni dandan ki ga meitte kita yo.

I'm getting bummed just listening to you.

☞ *ki ga shizumu* 気が沈む, *ki ga heru* 気が減る, *ki ga omoi* 気が重い

ki ga momeru 気が揉める *ki gets crumpled*

■ be anxious (to find out about something), wring *one's* hands (over something)

❏ 結果がどうなったか気が揉めるんだが、こちらから聞くわけにもいかないしね。

Kekka ga dō natta ka ki ga momeru n' da ga, kochira kara kiku wake ni mo ikanai shi ne.

I'm anxious to find out how things turned out, but I can't very well ask, now can I?

❏ 昨日は例の件で気が揉めて、一日中何も手につかなかったよ。

Kinō wa rei no ken de ki ga momete, ichinichi-jū nani mo te ni tsuka-nakatta yo.

Yesterday I was so worried about you-know-what that I didn't get a thing done all day.

➡ki o momu 気を揉む *crumple ki*

■ be anxious; fret, fuss, stew, worry

❏ 君が気を揉むのも無理はないが、連絡があるまで待つよりしかたないだろう。

Kimi ga ki o momu no mo muri wa nai ga, renraku ga aru made matsu yori shikata nai darō.

It's understandable that you'd be sweating things out, but there's not much you can do except wait for them to contact you.

❏ お父さんが気を揉んでもどうしようもないんだから、少し落ち着いたら。

Otōsan ga ki o monde mo dō shiyō mo nai n' da kara, sukoshi ochi-tsuitara.

It's not going to do you any good to get all worked up, Dad. Why don't you just try to relax?

❑ まったくいくつになっても親に気を揉ませる娘だ。

Mattaku ikutsu ni natte mo oya ni ki o momaseru musume da.

When are you going to start acting your age so your parents don't have to worry about you all the time?

ki ga yasashii 気が優しい *ki* is gentle

■ compassionate, gentle, kind, nice, sweet, warm

❑ 北嶋医院の看護婦さんはみんな美人で気が優しい。

Kitajima-iin no kangofu-san wa minna bijin de ki ga yasashii.

All the nurses at the Kitajima Clinic are good-looking, and nice too.

❑ 「気は優しくて力持ち」なんて桃太郎みたいな人だね。

"Ki wa yasashikute chikara-mochi" nante Momotarō mitai na hito da ne.

"Gentle-natured and strong," huh—sounds like [that legendary boy born from a peach] Momotaro or something.

❑ 気の優しい息子で、いつも私のことを心配してくれる。

Ki no yasashii musuko de, itsumo watashi no koto o shinpai shite kureru.

My son's so considerate, always thinking of me.

ki ga yasumaru 気が休まる *ki* rests

■ recharge *one's* batteries, relax, rest, take a breather, unwind

❑ 康子さんといる時だけは気が休まる。

Yasuko-san to iru toki dake wa ki ga yasumaru.

The only time I can really unwind is when I'm with Yasuko.

❑ 毎日毎日仕事に追われて気の休まる暇もない。

Mainichi-mainichi shigoto ni owarete ki no yasumaru hima mo nai.

It's just work, work, work every day, with no time to even catch my breath.

❑ 騒々しくて全然気の休まらない喫茶店だったね。

Sōzōshikute zenzen ki no yasumaranai kissa-ten datta ne.

With all the racket going on, that coffee shop was certainly no place to relax.

⇨ *hotto suru* ホッとする

➡️ki o yasumeru 気を休める rest *ki*

■ kick back, relax, rest

❑ しばらく休暇でもとって気を休める必要があると医者に言われた。

Shibaraku kyūka de mo totte ki o yasumeru hitsuyō ga aru to isha ni iwareta.

The doctor told me that I ought to take some time off and get a little R&R.

❑ 一晩ゆっくり寝て気を休めなさい。話はそれからだ。

Hitoban yukkuri nete ki o yasumenasai. Hanashi wa sore kara da.

Relax and get a good night's sleep. We can talk after that.

As with other such idioms with either ~ ga or ~ o, the distinction between *ki ga yasumaru* and *ki o yasumeru* is one of intentionality. Neither should be confused with *ki ga raku ni naru* 気が楽になる or *ki o raku ni suru* 気を楽にする, which mean to "relax" as from a state of nervous agitation. The idioms in this entry are used of a condition of reduced mental activity or stress and the resulting relaxation and refer to a psychological state, although this state is often accompanied by physical inactivity.

➡️kiyasume 気休め a *ki* rest

■ [empty] comfort, consolation, encouragement, reassurance, solace

❑ 単なる気休めと分かってはいるが、何かしないではいられないんだ。

Tannaru kiyasume to wakatte wa iru ga, nanika shinai de wa irarenai n' da.

I know it's only for my own peace of mind, but I can't just stand by and do nothing.

❑ そんな気休めはもう聞きあきたんだろう。

Sonna kiyasume wa mō kikiakita n' darō.

You've gotta be sick and tired of everybody patting you on the back, telling you things will be all right.

❑ 気休めばかり言わないで本当のことを教えて下さい。

Kiyasume bakari iwanai de hontō no koto o oshiete kudasai.

I want the truth, not a pat on the back. / Don't just tell me everything's going to be all right. Give it to me straight.

❑ 試験が始まるまでの間、気休めに単語カードをもう一度見直した。

Shiken ga hajimaru made no aida, kiyasume ni tango-kādo o mō ichido minaoshita.

I spent the time until the test began looking over my word cards one more time just to reassure myself.

❑ 海外旅行に出かける前に、気休めに英会話教室に通っている。

Kaigai ryokō ni dekakeru mae ni, kiyasume ni ei-kaiwa kyōshitsu ni ka-yotte iru.

She's going to an English conversation school before she goes abroad, just to ease her mind.

Say there's something that's got you wringing your hands, but you know there's nothing you can do that will really improve matters. You've just got to do *something*. Doing something will at least allow your *ki* to relax (*ki ga yasumaru*). That *something* is a *kiyasume*. When used in reference to a comment by another person, the expression is replete with negativity, expressing an awareness of how hollow the comment is.

---

ki ga yurumu   気が緩む   *ki* loosens

■ drop *one's* guard, let *one's* guard down, let up, relax

❐ ふっと気が緩む瞬間があるんだ。

Futto ki ga yurumu shunkan ga aru n' da.

There's always a moment when you lower your guard (without realizing it). / You can't stay on top of things every second.

❐ 酒で気が緩んで、本音が出てしまった。

Sake de ki ga yurunde, honne ga dete shimatta.

The drink loosened my tongue, and before I knew it I'd spoken my mind.

❐ こんな初歩的なミスをするなんて、気が緩んでるぞ。

Konna shoho-teki na misu o suru nante ki ga yurunde 'ru zo.

Your mind's not on what you're doing, making a simple mistake like this.

ki o yurumeru   気を緩める   loosen *one's ki*

■ ease off, let up, relax

❐ 気を緩めるつもりはなかったが、どうも疲れが出たようだ。

Ki o yurumeru tsumori wa nakatta ga, dōmo tsukare ga deta yō da.

I never intended to let up, but I guess I must have just been tired or something. / I didn't mean to be careless, but, you know, I was tired and all.

❐ 気を緩めないで、もっと真面目にやれ。

Ki o yurumenai de, motto majime ni yare.

Quit goofing off! Pay attention to what you're doing.

☞ *ki o nuku* 気を抜く

Whereas the previous entry (*ki ga yasumaru* 気が休まる) and its cognate *ki o yasumeru* 気を休める are used to describe an action thought to be required for good mental health and therefore carry positive connotations, *ki ga yurumu* and *ki o yurumeru* (together with their synonyms *ki ga nukeru* 気が抜ける and *ki o nuku* 気を抜く) are used of a relaxation incompatible with whatever activity is presently being undertaken and carry negative connotations. The activity may be driving, attending a meeting, or working, something which, in any case, requires ones full attention. As with other ~ *ga* and ~ *o* constructions, the latter indicates that the action is controllable by the agent, while the former indicates the opposite—namely that what happens is beyond control.

☞ *ki ga nukeru* 気が抜ける(#1)

ki ga yowaru 気が弱る *ki* weakens

■ lose *one's* zest for life, slow down, weaken

❐ 病気の時は誰だって気が弱るものですよ。

Byōki no toki wa dare datte ki ga yowaru mono desu yo.

I don't care who you are, getting sick is bound to take a something out of you (take some of the fun out of life).

❐ 僕も最近歳のせいかずいぶんと気が弱ってきちゃってねえ。

Boku mo saikin toshi no sei ka zuibun to ki ga yowatte kichatte nē.

I don't know if it's age or what, but I don't look forward to getting up in the morning nearly as much as I used to.

ki ga yowai 気が弱い *ki* is weak

■ be fainthearted, meek, timid, unassertive, weak-kneed, weak-willed; be a pussycat, a pushover

❐ 気が弱くて、「いや」と言えないでキャッチ・セールスにひっかかった。

Ki ga yowakute, "iya" to ienai de kyatchi-sērusu ni hikkakatta.

I'm such a weenie I can't even bring myself to say no to those high-pressure salesmen that buttonhole you on the street.

❐ 面接にやってきたのは40代後半の気の弱そうな男性だった。

Mensetsu ni yatte kita no wa yonjū-dai kōhan no ki no yowasō na dansei datta.

The guy who showed up for the interview was some wimpy-looking guy in his late forties.

also *kiyowai* 気弱い [in front of a noun]
☞ *ki ga chiisai* 気が小さい
☛ *ki ga tsuyoi* 気が強い

➡*yowaki (na)* 弱気(な) weak *ki*

■ gutless, irresolute, spineless, timid, weak-kneed

❑ 断られるのが怖いなんて、そんな弱気なことでどうするんだ。

Kotowarareru no ga kowai nante, sonna yowaki na koto de dō suru n' da.

How are you going to get anywhere if you're always quaking in your boots because you think you'll be turned down?

❑ 彼の場合は慎重というより弱気ですよ。

Kare no bāi wa shinchō to iu yori yowaki desu yo.

In his case, he's not so much cautious as downright timid.

also *kiyowa na* 気弱な
☛ *tsuyoki (na)* 強気(な) (see under *ki ga tsuyoi* 気が強い)

ki ga raku ni naru 気が楽になる *one's ki* relaxes

■ be a relief, be relieved, feel better, feel like a weight has been lifted from *one's* shoulders, feel lighthearted, feel relieved

❑ 本当のことを話せば気が楽になるよ。

Hontō no koto o hanaseba ki ga raku ni naru yo.

You'll feel a whole lot better if you just tell us what really happened. / It'll be a relief if you just tell the truth.

❑ 今年の確定申告も終わって、気が楽になったなあ。

Kotoshi no kakutei-shinkoku mo owatte, ki ga raku ni natta nā.

What a load off my mind it is to have finished filing this year's tax return and all.

❑ 気が楽になったら急にお腹がすいてきた。

Ki ga raku ni nattara kyū ni onaka ga suite kita.

With that off my mind, I got hungry all of a sudden.

➡ki o raku ni suru 気を楽にする relax *one's ki*

■ relax, make *oneself* at home

❑ 気を楽にするために何回か深呼吸してみた。

Ki o raku ni suru tame ni nankai ka shin-kokyū shite mita.

I took several deep breaths to try and relax.

❑ そこへ横になって気を楽にしてください。

Soko e yoko ni natte ki o raku ni shite kudasai.

Lie down there and relax, please.

☞ *ki o raku ni motsu* 気を楽に持つ (see under *ki o ~ motsu* 気を～持つ)

➡ **ki ga raku (na)** 気が楽(な) easy *ki*

■ [of a person] be relieved, feel lighthearted; [of a condition] easy, a snap, a piece of cake, no sweat; a relief

❑ 今度のプロジェクトほど気が楽な仕事は珍しい。

Kondo no purojekuto hodo ki ga raku na shigoto wa mezurashii.

Jobs as easy as this project are few and far between.

❑ 林さんならよく知っているから気が楽だよ。

Hayashi-san nara yoku shitte iru kara ki ga raku da yo.

If it's Ms. Hayashi, it won't be a big deal because I know her quite well.

➡ **kiraku na** 気楽な easy *ki*

■ [of a person] carefree, easy-going, happy-go-lucky, laid-back; [of a condition] can handle it, comfortable, no complaints

❑ お前も気楽な奴だな、まったく。

Omae mo kiraku na yatsu da na, mattaku.

You're one laid-back kind of guy, aren't you.

❑ 定年後は気楽な隠居生活で、子供たちから「サンデー毎日」*と冷やかされている。

Teinen-go wa kiraku na inkyo-seikatsu de, kodomo-tachi kara "Sandē Mainichi" to hiyakasarete iru.

I've got to put up with the kids teasing me about living the life of Riley now that I'm comfortably retired.

　　* *"Sandē Mainichi"*: a play on the name of a weekly magazine and the fact that, for the man in our sentence, virtually everyday (*mainichi*) is Sunday

❑ そんなに堅いこと言わないで、もっと気楽にやりましょうよ。

Sonna ni katai koto iwanai de, motto kiraku ni yarimashō yo.

Quit being so difficult. Let's just take it easy, OK.

❑ 独り者は気楽でいいね。

Hitorimono wa kiraku de ii ne.

Must be great being footloose and fancy-free.

　　☞ *nonki na* 呑気な

ki ga wakai 気が若い *ki* is young

■ young at heart

❑ おじいちゃんはいくつになっても気が若いね。

Ojīchan wa ikutsu ni natte mo ki ga wakai ne.

It doesn't matter how old you get, Grandpa, you'll always be young at heart.

❐ 気だけは若いが体力の方はもうだめだ。

Ki dake wa wakai ga tairyoku no hō wa mō dame da.

I feel young at heart, but the old body is going downhill fast. / The spirit is willing but the flesh is weak.

kigurai 気位 rank of *ki*

■ pride, self-esteem, self-respect; arrogance, vanity; be stuck up, think *one's* shit doesn't stink

❐ あいつエリートだという気位ばかりで、実力は全然ないさ。

Aitsu erīto da to iu kigurai bakari de, jitsuryoku wa zenzen nai sa.

He's as proud as can be about being a member of the "elite," but he absolutely worthless on the job.

❐ 家柄を鼻にかけた気位の高い人で、私は好きになれない。

Iegara o hana ni kaketa kigurai no takai hito de, watashi wa suki ni narenai.

She's all wrapped up in how great her pedigree is and all. I haven't got any use for her, though.

kigurō 気苦労 hard work for *ki*

■ anxiety, care, mental anguish, pains, worry

❐ 出世コースに乗ったら乗ったで、人には言えない気苦労があるらしいよ。

Shusse-kōsu ni nottara notta de, hito ni wa ienai kigurō ga aru rashii yo.

Once you're on the fast track, you come under a lot of strain that you can never really explain to others.

❐ 結構気苦労の多い職場みたい。

Kekkō kigurō no ōi shokuba mitai.

It sounds like a workplace where you've got to worry a lot about interpersonal relations.

❐ 京子も家の中がいざこざ続きで、気苦労が絶えないんですって。

Kyōko mo ie no naka ga izakoza-tsuzuki de, kigurō ga taenai n' desu tte.

According to Kyoko, all the hassles at home are a constant source of concern (worry) for her.

❐ おふくろと女房の間に挟まって気苦労してるぜ、まったく。

Ofukuro to nyōbō no aida ni hasamatte kigurō shite 'ru ze, mattaku.

Hey, man, let me tell you, being caught between my mother and my old lady is wearing me out (is no fun).

kigokoro 気心 *ki* heart

■ *one's* feelings, *one's* heart and mind, *one's* innermost thoughts

❐ やっぱり学生時代のお友だちがいちばん気心が分かってるわ。

Yappari gakusei-jidai no otomodachi ga ichiban kigokoro ga wakatte 'ru wa.

I swear, there's no one who can really understand you like an old schoolmate.

❐ 気心の知れた友人とは、しばらく会ってなくてもすぐ話が弾むもんだね。

Kigokoro no shireta yūjin to wa, shibaraku atte 'nakute mo sugu hanashi ga hazumu mon da ne.

It's amazing how really good friends who haven't met for a while can find all kinds of things to talk about when they do get together.

❐ 中井さんっていつまでたっても気心の知れない人だなあ。

Nakai-san tte itsu made tatte mo kigokoro no shirenai hito da nā.

Nakai is someone you can just never seem to get close to (get to know).

Anyone about whom you would use *kigokoro no shireta* about is, of course, a *ki no okenai hito* 気の置けない人. Er, that is unless we're talking about those teenagers busily redefining the term. They'll drive you up the wall. See the note at *ki ga okenai.*

---

kikotsu 気骨 a boned *ki*

■ [〜がある] (have) backbone, (have the strength of *one's*) convictions

❐ 上田君は今時の学生には珍しく気骨があるな。

Ueda-kun wa imadoki no gakusei ni wa mezurashiku kikotsu ga aru na.

Ueda's not like most students these days; he's actually got covictions.

❐ なかなか気骨のある人物じゃないか。

Nakanaka kikotsu no aru jinbutsu ja nai ka.

He's got real backbone.

❐ 頑固なのも困るが、お前たちには気骨がなさ過ぎるぞ。

Ganko na no mo komaru ga, omae-tachi ni wa kikotsu ga nasasugiru zo.

I'm not saying you've got to be stubborn, but you guys are far too wishy-washy.

By convention *kikotsu ga aru* is not used in reference to women. The idiom itself is not sexist; rather, usage reflects the fact that historically women have not been in positions requiring (encouraging?) them to express their views. The consensus of the authors is that when a woman sticks by her guns, however praiseworthy that effort may be, words like *kachiki* and *namaiki* (both of which are included in this book) would be used, suggesting that it is not her place to have an opinion, much less to defend it.

The characters 気骨 have a variant reading, *kibone*, with a different meaning, "anxiety" or "pains." This word is most commonly found in the phrase *kibone ga oreru* 気骨が折れる, which means to be emotionally exhausted or "worn to a frazzle." It is derived by adding *ki* to the expression *hone ga oreru* 骨が折れる, which literally means "break a bone."

➤ 中間管理職は想像していた以上に気骨が折れるよ。
Chūkan-kanrishoku wa sōzō shite ita ijō ni kibone ga oreru yo.
Being in middle management takes a lot more out of you than I ever thought it would.

☞ *kigurō o suru* 気苦労をする (see under *kigurō*), *kizukare* 気疲れ

kisaku (na) 気さく(な) free *ki*

■ easy to get along with, laid-back, natural, relaxed, unaffected

☐ 有名人なのに偉ぶらない気さくな方ですね。
Yūmei-jin na no ni eraburanai kisaku na kata desu ne.
She's very unassuming and easy-going for a celebrity, isn't she.

☐ 彼とは気さくに話ができるから、飲みに行っても楽しい。
Kare to wa kisaku ni hanashi ga dekiru kara, nomi ni itte mo tanoshii.
It's fun to go out for a drink with him because he's so easy to talk to.

☐ もっと気さくに誰とでも話せる性格になりたいよ。
Motto kisaku ni dare to de mo hanaseru seikaku ni naritai yo.
I wish I had the kind of personality that lets you talk openly to all kinds of people.

☞ *kigaru (na)* 気軽(な) (see under *ki ga karui* 気が軽い)

kizetsu suru 気絶する cut off *ki*

■ black out, faint, fall unconscious

☐ 幸い気絶しただけで怪我はなかったんです。
Saiwai kizetsu shita dake de kega wa nakatta n' desu.
Fortunately, I just fainted and wasn't injured at all.

❒ 金額を聞いて気絶しそうになったよ。

Kingaku o kiite kizetsu shisō ni natta yo.

I nearly passed out when I heard how much it was.

A noun form of *kizetsu* also exists but is virtually never encountered.

☞ *ki ga tōku naru* 気が遠くなる, *ki o ushinau* 気を失う

kizewashii 気ぜわしい *ki* busy

■ be harried, hounded, in a tizzy, in a dither; feel rushed; be restless

❒ ぎりぎりまで寝てるから、朝はいつも気ぜわしいんだ。

Girigiri made nete 'ru kara, asa wa itsumo kizewashii n' da.

I like to sleep till the last minute, so I'm always running around like mad (a chicken with its head cut off) in the morning.

❒ 気ぜわしく机の上を片づけて、飛ぶように帰って行った。

Kizewashiku tsukue no ue o katazukete, tobu yō ni kaette itta.

He hurriedly straightened up his desk and then flew out the door.

⇨ *isogashii* 忙しい, *sewashii* 忙しい (same *kanji*), *awatadashii* 慌ただ しい

kidate 気立て *ki* standing

■ disposition, nature, temperament

❒ 気立てがいい娘さんで、近所でも評判がいいですよ。

Kidate ga ii musume-san de, kinjo de mo hyōban ga ii desu yo.

She's so sweet (good-natured) that everyone in the neighborhood likes her.

❒ 気立てがやさしい子で、迷い犬や捨て猫を見ると放っておけないら しい。

Kidate ga yasashii ko de, mayoi-inu ya sute-neko o miru to hōtte okenai rashii.

She's so kindhearted that she has to take care of every lost dog and stray cat she comes across.

Generally used of a person's nature when it is thought to be good, *kidate* is never used in conjunction with negative words or phrases.

⇨ *kishō* 気性, *kishitsu* 気質

kizukau 気遣う use *ki*

■ be careful (not to hurt *someone's* feelings), be considerate, think of, think about, worry (about), have *someone's* best interests at heart

❏ 彼はいつも「君はどう思うの？」と、相手のことを気遣う。

Kare wa itsumo "Kimi wa dō omou no?" to, aite no koto o kizukau.

He's quite considerate of others, always asking, "What do you think?"

❏ 仕事も大切だろうが、もっと家族を気遣ってあげればいいのにね。

Shigoto mo taisetsu darō ga, motto kazoku o kizukatte agereba ii no ni ne.

Work's important, all right, but it'd be nice if he'd worry a little more about his family, too.

❏ 妊娠中は、体を気遣ってきちんと一日三食取らなければならない。

Ninshin-chū wa, karada o kizukatte kichin to ichinichi-sanshoku toranakereba naranai.

You've got to be careful to eat three meals a day and pay attention to your health when you're pregnant.

❏ 彼のことを気遣うあまりに他の人の気持ちに無神経だった。

Kare no koto o kizukau amari ni hoka no hito no kimochi ni mu-shinkei datta.

I was so wrapped up in him that I was oblivious to how other people felt.

❏ 気遣ったつもりで遠慮してかえって相手を傷つけてしまった。

Kizukatta tsumori de enryo shite kaette aite o kizutsukete shimatta.

I tried to take his feelings into consideration and not be pushy, but I ended him hurting him all the same.

❏ がっかりしている父を気遣って母は努めて明るく振る舞っている。

Gakkari shite iru chichi o kizukatte haha wa tsutomete akaruku furumatte iru.

Dad is all bummed out, so Mom is doing what she can to cheer him up. / Mom is all smiles trying to cheer Dad up.

❏ 娘のことを気遣ってやったのにちっとも感謝しない。

Musume no koto o kizukatte yatta no ni chittomo kansha shinai.

I had my daughter's best interests at heart, but she doesn't show any gratitude at all.

Kizukau is used when closeness to and affection for others underlies one's concern. It is distinguished from *ki o kubaru*, which is the effort one undertakes more in response to another's perceived need than from any particular affection for that person. *Ki o tsukau*, on the other hand, is used of actions taken for another's benefit that do not come straight from the heart and therefore can easily become an emotional burden.

☞ *ki o tsukau* 気を使う, *ki o kubaru* 気を配る, *ki ni kakeru* 気にかける, *ki ni suru* 気にする

⇨ *daiji ni suru* 大事にする, *shinpai suru* 心配する

➡**kizukai** 気遣い *ki* handling

1. anxiety, concern, fear, worry; (take) care (not to hurt *someone's* feelings), consideration, regard, solicitude

❒ 朝が早い母への気遣いから夜はテレビの音を小さくすることにしている。

Asa ga hayai haha e no kizukai kara yoru wa terebi no oto o chiisaku suru koto ni shite iru.

Out of consideration for my mother, who has to get up early in the morning, I'm keeping the TV turned down at night.

❒ 私の気遣いは彼にはまったく汲んでもらえなかった。

Watashi no kizukai wa kare ni wa mattaku kunde moraenakatta.

He didn't give any consideration to all the care I had taken on his behalf. / Nothing I did for him even registered.

2. [in the negative] no chance of, no risk of

❒ この様子じゃ雨が降る気遣いはなさそうだな。

Kono yōsu ja ame ga furu kizukai wa nasasō da na.

By the looks of things, there's no danger of it raining, I guess.

❒ あいつなら人に騙される気遣いはないさ。

Aitsu nara hito ni damasareru kizukai wa nai sa.

You don't have to worry about him ever getting taken in by anyone (having the wool pulled over his eyes).

See note at *kikubari* 気配り for the distinction between it and *kizukai*.

☞ *kigane* 気兼ね

kizukare 気疲れ tired *ki*

■ mental fatigue, nervous exhaustion

❒ 転職してからこっち気疲れの連続で、少し酒の量が増えたかも知れないなあ。

Tenshoku shite kara kotchi kizukare no renzoku de, sukoshi sake no ryō ga fueta kamo shirenai nā.

It's just been one thing after another since I changed jobs, and I'm emotionally beat (drained). I may even be drinking a little more, too.

❐ 姉貴の結婚式の後、おふくろ気疲れで 2 、 3 日寝込んだんだ。

Aneki no kekkon-shiki no ato, ofukuro kizukare de ni-san-nichi nekonda n' da.

Mom was worn to a frazzle after my older sister's wedding and ended up in bed for for a couple days.

❐ あんまり張り切ると気疲れするんじゃないかい。

Anmari harikiru to kizukare suru n' ja nai kai.

Don't you think you ought to cool it a little bit? You're pretty wound up.

❐ 体は全然疲れてないのに、すっかり気疲れしちゃったみたい。

Karada wa zenzen tsukarete nai no ni, sukkari kizukare shichatta mitai.

I'm not a bit tired physically. I guess it's just nervous exhaustion.

☞ *kibone ga oreru* 気骨が折れる (see under *kikotsu* 気骨)

ki de ki o yamu 気で気を病む *ki* gets ill due to *ki*

■ get all worked up about nothing, work *oneself* into a lather, worry *oneself* sick (unnecessarily)

❐ 彼女の場合は世間体を気にし過ぎて、「気で気を病む」の見本みたいなもんだ。

Kanojo no bāi wa seken-tei o ki ni shisugite, "ki de ki o yamu" no mihon mitai na mon da.

The way she's so uptight about appearances and all, she's your classic worrywart.

❐ 気で気を病むということもありますから、あまり思い詰めない方がいいですよ。

Ki de ki o yamu to iu koto mo arimasu kara, amari omoitsumenai hō ga ii desu yo.

You know what they say about worrying yourself sick about nothing. If I were you, I'd try not to take things to heart so much.

The sense of the idiom is that by taking something too much to heart, *ki ni shisugite* 気にしすぎて, one can become psychologically distressed.

☞ *yamai wa ki kara* 病は気から

kidoru 気取る to take *ki*

1. act big; be affected, conceited, fake, phony, pompous; put on airs

❏ たまには気取って二人で高級レストランへ行くのも楽しいものだよ。

Tama ni wa kidotte futari de kōkyū resutoran e iku no mo tanoshii mono da yo.

It's fun sometimes to put on the dog and go out to an expensive restaurant.

❏ 何よ！ 気取って！

Nani yo! Kidotte!

You must really think you're something! / Who do you think you are?

Anyone who fits the above descriptions is a *kidori-ya* 気取り屋.

---

2. pass *oneself* off as, pretend to be, pose as

❏ 彼は改革派を気取りながらいち早く寝返った。

Kare wa kaikaku-ha o kidorinagara ichi-hayaku negaetta.

He made like he was a reformer and all, but he was the first to go over to the other side.

❏ 当時の私は物わかりの良い女を気取っていた。

Tōji no watashi wa monowakari no yoi onna o kidotte ita.

Back then I passed myself off as a worldly wise and sophisticated woman.

ki ni iru 気に入る come into *one's ki*

■ like, take a fancy to, take to

❏ この条件なら先方も気に入るでしょう。

Kono jōken nara senpō mo ki ni iru deshō.

I'm sure these conditions will be to their liking as well.

❏ 気に入ってもらえてうれしいよ。

Ki ni itte moraete ureshii yo.

I'm sure glad you like it.

❏ この子は気に入ったおもちゃを持たせておけば、何時間でもおとなしく遊んでくれるから助かります。

Kono ko wa ki ni itta omocha o motasete okeba, nanji-kan de mo otonashiku asonde kureru kara tasukarimasu.

It's great because if you give her a toy she likes she'll play with it quietly for hours.

❏ 父は気に入らない人とは話もしない。

Chichi wa ki ni iranai hito to wa hanashi mo shinai.

Dad won't even give the time of day to somebody he doesn't like.

➥oki ni mesu お気に召す take into *one's ki*

■ favor, like, look favorably upon

❒ お気に召す品がございましたか。

Oki ni mesu shina ga gozaimashita ka.

Were you able to find anything you liked?

❒ お気に召したらいくつでもどうぞ。

Oki ni meshitara ikutsu de mo dōzo.

If you find them to your liking, please feel free to take as many as you want.

❒ 鈴木さんはこの春の人事異動で田中さんが先に部長になったのがお気に召さないらしい。

Suzuki-san wa kono haru no jinji-idō de Tanaka-san ga saki ni buchō ni natta no ga oki ni mesanai rashii.

Suzuki isn't exactly jumping for joy now that Tanaka has been promoted ahead of him as a department head in this spring's reshuffling of personnel.

❒ 「お気に召すまま」見に行かない？　新しい演出だって。

"Oki ni mesu mama" mi ni ikanai? Atarashii enshutsu datte.

Do you want to go see *As You Like It*? It's supposed to be a new interpretation.

Oki ni mesu is the honorific form of *ki ni iru*.

➥oki-ni-iri お気に入り

■ favorite, pet, the apple of one's eye

❒ あいつは先生のお気に入りだから、さぼっても大丈夫さ。

Aitsu wa sensei no oki-ni-iri da kara, sabotte mo daijōbu sa.

Since he's the teacher's pet he can get away with cutting class.

❒ これが彼女のお気に入りの香水らしい。

Kore ga kanojo no oki-ni-iri no kōsui rashii.

This seems to be her favorite perfume.

Compared with *suki na*, *ki ni itta*, or *ki ni itte iru*, *oki-ni-iri* generally expresses a stronger sense of liking—something akin to "loving" perhaps. When casting about for an appropriate way to say "my favorite … " in Japanese, it is usually safer to go with "*watakushi no suki na …* " or "*watakushi no ki ni itte iru … ,*" for although "*watakushi no oki-ni-iri … *" is not always inappropriate, it has a childish ring for many Japanese.

☛ *ki ni kuwanai* 気に食わない

ki ni kakaru 気にかかる hang on *ki*

■ be bothered by, concerned about; have *something* on *one's* mind, think about, worry (about)

❒ 内緒だけど夫より猫の健康の方が気にかかるのよ。

Naisho da kedo otto yori neko no kenkō no hō ga ki ni kakaru no yo.

Just between you and me, I worry more about my cat's health than my husband's.

❒ 試合の結果が気にかかって、早く会議が終わらないかとばかり思っていた。

Shiai no kekka ga ki ni kakatte, hayaku kaigi ga owaranai ka to bakari omotte ita.

The outcome of the game was on my mind so much that all I could think of was how soon the meeting would end.

Believe it or not, there is a subtle distinction to be made between this and *ki ni kakeru* (see below). *Ki ni kakeru* is usually used after the fact or source of immediate concern has passed to indicate that concern lingers, while *ki ni kakaru* is more immediate.

☞ *ki ni naru* 気になる

⇨ *shinpai ni naru* 心配になる

➡kigakari 気がかり *something* hanging on *one's* ki

■ a concern, headache, worry; something on *one's* mind

❒ 入院している母がたったひとつの気がかりです。

Nyūin shite iru haha ga tatta hitotsu no kigakari desu.

The only thing that bothers me is my mother in the hospital.

❒ 売り上げが伸び悩んでいるのが気がかりだ。

Uriage ga nobinayande iru no ga kigakari da.

I'm a little worried about the sluggish sales.

❒ 西田さんの気がかりはアメリカへ留学している娘らしい。

Nishida-san no kigakari wa Amerika e ryūgaku shite iru musume rashii.

Nishida's chief concern (big worry) is apparently the safety of his daughter who's studying in the United States.

⇨ *shinpai* 心配

➡kigakari (na) 気がかり(な) a *ki* hanging

■ bothersome, troubling, worrisome

❒ 決して気がかりな相手ではなかった。

Kesshite kigakari na aite de wa nakatta.

As an opponent, he wasn't worth losing a night's sleep over.

❒ 今いちばん気がかりなことは夫の働き過ぎです。

Ima ichiban kigakari na koto wa otto no hatarakisugi desu.

What's bothering me most now is my husband working too hard for his own good.

> ☞ *ki ni naru* 気になる
>
> ⇨ *shinpai (na)* 心配(な)

➡ki ni kakeru 気にかける hang *something* on *one's ki*

■ be concerned about, worry about

❑ 母は私のことを気にかけるあまり、毎日2回も電話をよこす。

Haha wa watashi no koto o ki ni kakeru amari, mainichi nikai mo denwa o yokosu.

My mother is so worried about me that she calls twice a day.

❑ 僕の健康を気にかけてくれるのはありがたいが、仕事のことには口を出さないでほしい。

Boku no kenkō o ki ni kakete kureru no wa arigatai ga, shigoto no koto ni wa kuchi o dasanai de hoshii.

It's nice that you worry so much about my health and all, but I'd really appreciate it if you'd not tell me how to do my job.

See note under *ki ni kakaru*.

> ☞ *ki ni suru* 気にする
>
> ⇨ *shinpai suru* 心配する

ki ni kuwanai 気に食わない not eaten by *ki*

■ don't like, don't care (much) for, dislike, get on *one's* nerves, go against the grain, have no use for, make *one* sick, rub *one* the wrong way

❑ 俺はそもそもあいつの顔が気に食わねぇ。

Ore wa somosomo aitsu no kao ga ki ni kuwanē.

Can't stand the fucker's looks in the first place.

❑ 新入りのくせにでかい態度で気に食わない野郎だぜ。

Shin-iri no kuse ni dekai taido de ki ni kuwanai yarō da ze.

The new guy makes me sick the way he swaggers around like owned the place.

Much rougher and more vulgar than *ki ni iranai*. There is no affirmative of the *ki ni kuwanai* form.

> ☞ *ki ni iranai* 気に入らない (see under *ki ni iru* 気に入る)
>
> ☛ *ki ni iru* 気に入る

ki ni sawaru 気に障(触)る to touch *ki*

■ annoy, bother, get to *one*, irritate

❒ あいつの一言一言が気に障る。
Aitsu no hitokoto hitokoto ga ki ni sawaru.
Every little thing he says gets on my nerves.

❒ いったい何が谷川さんの気に障ったんだろう。
Ittai nani ga Tanikawa-san no ki ni sawatta n' darō.
I wonder just what it was that rubbed Ms. Tanikawa the wrong way.

❒ 正直に言います。お気に障ったらお許し下さい。
Shōjiki ni iimasu. Oki ni sawattara oyurushi kudasai.
I'll be frank, and I hope you'll forgive me if what I say offends you.

ki ni suru 気にする make into *ki*

■ be bothered by, care, have *something* on *one's* mind, let *something* get to *one*, mind, pay attention to, take *something* to heart

❒ 彼のこと気にしないで。
Kare no koto ki ni shinai de.
Forget him! / Don't let him bother you!

❒ 気にすんなよ*。
Ki ni sun' na yo.
Don't sweat it, man! / Hang loose!
   * *sun' na*: a contraction of *suru na*

❒ あの人に言われたことなんて気にすることはないよ。
Ano hito ni iwareta koto nante ki ni suru koto wa nai yo.
Don't worry about what he says. / Don't let anything he says bother you.

❒ 体重を気にして、コーヒーはブラックで飲んでいる。
Taijū o ki ni shite, kōhī wa burakku de nonde iru.
I drink my coffee black because I'm watching my weight.

❒ この間のことは気にしていませんから忘れてください。
Kono aida no koto wa ki ni shite imasen kara wasurete kudasai.
What happened the other day is water under the bridge as far as I'm concerned (I'm not going to make an issue of what happened the other day), so just forget it.

❒ 鹿は人間を気にする様子もなくゆっくり歩いていった。
Shika wa ningen o ki ni suru yōsu mo naku yukkuri aruite itta.
The deer was ambling along and didn't appear at all concerned about the people.

❏ 学生は授業が終わる時間を気にして時計ばかり見ている。

Gakusei wa jugyō ga owaru jikan o ki ni shite tokei bakari mite iru.

The students are doing nothing but looking at their watches, the main thing on their minds being when the class will end.

❏ 田中の奴、鈴木さんを気にしてカッコつけてるんだ。

Tanaka no yatsu, Suzuki-san o ki ni shite kakko tsuke 'ru n' da.

Tanaka's acting cool 'cause he's got the hots for Suzuki.

☞ *ki ni naru* 気になる, *ki ni tomeru* 気に止める (the latter is not a synonym for last two examples)

ki ni tomeru 気に止める　stop in *ki*

■ be aware of, notice, occur to, pay attention to, bear in mind

❏ 最初は通りの暗さを気に止めていなかったが、だんだん不安になった。

Saisho wa tōri no kurasa o ki ni tomete inakatta ga, dandan fuan ni natta.

At first it didn't register just how dark the street was, but pretty soon I got nervous about it.

❏ こうした*問題をまったく気に止めていないようだ。

Kōshita mondai o mattaku ki ni tomete inai yō da.

None of these problems appears to affect him in the slightest.

* *kōshita*: = *kono yō na*

❏ 年寄りの言うことも少しは気に止めるものだ。

Toshiyori no iu koto mo sukoshi wa ki ni tomeru mono da.

You can't entirely ignore what old folks say.

❏ これだけは気に止めて、くれぐれも無茶なことはするな。

Kore dake wa ki ni tomete, kuregure mo mucha na koto wa suru na.

There's one thing I want you to bear in mind: whatever you do, don't go overboard.

❏ 標識を気に止めないで走っていたら道に迷ってしまったよ。

Hyōshiki o ki ni tomenai de hashitte itara michi ni mayotte shimatta yo.

I was just going along on my merry way, not paying any attention to the road signs, and I ended up getting lost.

☞ *ki ni suru* 気にする

ki ni naru 気になる　become *ki*

■ bother, be bothered by, be (have *something*) on *one's* mind, be disturbing, be (get) on *one's* nerves, wonder about, worry about, be worrying

❏ きちょうめんな人だから壁の絵がちょっと曲がっても気になるらしい。

Kichōmen na hito da kara kabe no e ga chotto magatte mo ki ni naru rashii.

He's such a stickler for detail that if there's a picture on the wall that's even a little bit cockeyed, it bothers him.

❏ 隣の部屋の話し声が気になって勉強できない。

Tonari no heya no hanashigoe ga ki ni natte benkyō dekinai.

I can't study with all the jabbering going on next door.

❏ 気にしている素振りはみせないが、内心気になっているに違いない。

Ki ni shite iru soburi wa misenai ga, naishin ki ni natte iru ni chigainai.

He may act as if it's nothing, but down deep it's got to be getting to him.

❏ 今日の試合が気になってゆうべはよく眠れなかった。

Kyō no shiai ga ki ni natte yūbe wa yoku nemurenakatta.

I couldn't sleep last night thinking about the game today.

❏ 彼女の欠点も気にならないどころかかえって可愛いぐらいだ。

Kanojo no ketten mo ki ni naranai dokoro ka kaette kawaii gurai da.

I not only don't mind her foibles, I actually think they're kind of cute.

❏ 彼女が別れ際に何を言おうとしたのか気になる。

Kanojo ga wakare-giwa ni nani o iō to shita no ka ki ni naru.

I can't help wondering what she was about to say just before we parted ways.

❏ ボロ車なので都心で走ると他人の目が気になる。

Boro-guruma na no de toshin de hashiru to tanin no me ga ki ni naru.

My car's such a junker that I get self-conscious when I'm driving downtown.

❏ まだ気になることが一つだけ残っている。

Mada ki ni naru koto ga hitotsu dake nokotte iru.

There's just one other thing that still bothers me.

❏ 美人の新入社員が気になって見積もり書の計算をまちがえた。

Bijin no shinnyū-shain ga ki ni natte mitsumori-sho no keisan o machi-gaeta.

I couldn't get my mind off the good-looking new woman in the office and ended up messing up the estimate I was working on.

❏ 宝くじの当選番号発表が気になって仕事が手につかない。

Takarakuji no tōsen-bangō ga ki ni natte shigoto ga te ni tsukanai.

I can't get any work done, thinking about what number is going to win the lottery.

❏ こうやって料理すればにんにくの臭いも気になりませんよ。

Kō yatte ryōri sureba ninniku no nioi mo ki ni narimasen yo.

If you cook it like this, the garlic odor won't bother you.

❑ 気になるお値段ですが、三枚組み特別価格は￥13、000でお買い得です。

Ki ni naru onedan desu ga, sanmai-gumi tokubetsu-kakaku wa ichiman-sanzen-kyūhyaku-en de okaidoku desu.

And now for what you have all been waiting for, our special, one-time-only price of ￥13,000 for a package of three.

☞ *ki ni suru* 気にする

ki ni yamu 気に病む to sicken *ki*

■ worry (needlessly) about, fret over, stew

❑ そんなこと気に病むなよ。

Sonna koto ki ni yamu na yo.

Don't let a silly thing like that bother you.

❑ 彼女は噂をよく気に病むたちなんだ。

Kanojo wa uwasa o yoku ki ni yamu tachi nan da.

She's the type that's always fretting about some rumor or other.

Similar to *ki ni suru,* but the person about whom it is used is much more deeply troubled, morbidly even, by the cause of concern.

☞ *ki ni suru* 気にする

ki no sei 気のせい because of *ki*

■ it's all in *one's* head (imagination), must be imagining things, be a figment of *one's* imagination

❑ 電話鳴らなかった？ 気のせいかな。

Denwa naranakatta? Ki no sei ka na.

Did the phone ring, or am I just imagining things?

❑ 近ごろときどき胸のあたりが痛むので医者へ行ったら気のせいだと言われた。藪医者め！

Chikagoro tokidoki mune no atari ga itamu no de isha e ittara ki no sei da to iwareta. Yabu-isha me!

You know, I've been having these chest pains lately so I went to the doctor, and you know what that quack told me? "It's all in your head."

❑ 太った人が暑がりなのは気のせいではなく、科学的根拠がある。

Futotta hito ga atsugari na no wa ki no sei de wa naku, kagaku-teki kon-kyo ga aru.

There's more to fat people feeling hot all the time than their imaginations; there's a scientific reason for it.

❑ 気のせいか、この人には貴族の風格が漂っている。

Ki no sei ka, kono hito ni wa kizoku no fūkaku ga tadayotte iru.

I don't know if it's all in my head or what, but there's something aristocratic about that person.

ki no doku (na)   気の毒(な)   poison of *ki*

■ pitiful, regrettable, sad, unfortunate

❑ お気の毒でしたね。

Oki no doku deshita ne.

That's too bad. / I'm sorry to hear that. / I'm so sorry.

❑ 地震の被災者の方々は本当にお気の毒ですね。

Jishin no hisai-sha no katagata wa hontō ni oki no doku desu ne.

It's really terrible (a pity) about the earthquake victims.

❑ あいつが首になったことなんか、気の毒でも何でもない。自業自得さ。

Aitsu ga kubi ni natta koto nanka, ki no doku de mo nan de mo nai. Jigō-jitoku sa.

I don't feel a bit sorry for him. It's his own fault he got the ax.

❑ 小山君には一人で責任を取らせてしまって気の毒なことをしたね。

Koyama-kun ni wa hitori de sekinin o torasete shimatte ki no doku na koto o shita ne.

It's regrettable that we had to let Koyama take all the blame for what happened.

❑ 山下さんは気の毒に8人の奥さんを次々に病気で亡くした。

Yamashita-san wa ki no doku ni hachinin no okusan o tsugitsugi ni byōki de nakushita.

Poor old Yamashita lost all eight of his wives to illness.

ki no mochiyō   気の持ちよう   way of holding *one's ki*

■ *one's* frame of mind, how one looks at it (things)

❑ 幸福か不幸かは最終的には本人の気の持ちようによるもんだ。

Kōfuku ka fukō ka wa saishū-teki ni wa honnin no ki no mochiyō ni yoru mon da.

Fortune or misfortune ultimately depend on how you look at things. / Whether a person is happy or not ultimately depends on how he views things.

❑ 気の持ちようひとつで人生180度変わるんですよ。

Ki no mochiyō hitotsu de jinsei hyakuhachijū-do kawaru n' desu yo.

A change in your frame of mind can completely turn your life around.

⇨ *kimochi no mochiyō* 気持ちの持ちよう

ki no yamai 気の病 illness of *ki*

■ an illness brought on by emotional fatigue, a psychosomatic illness, neurosis

❑ 家族からも気の病だと言われて相手にしてもらえない。

Kazoku kara mo ki no yamai da to iwarete aite ni shite moraenai.

Even my family tells me that it's all in my head and won't take me seriously.

❑ この患者さんは検査でも異常はないし、気の病の要素が強いから神経科受診を勧めた。

Kono kanja-san wa kensa de mo ijō wa nai shi, ki no yamai no yōso ga tsuyoi kara shinkei-ka jushin o susumeta.

Since nothing irregular showed up on the tests we ran on this patient and there is reason to believe his illness is largely psychosomatic, I recommended that he see someone in neurology.

ki wa kokoro 気は心 *ki* is heart

■ it's the thought that counts, a token of one's appreciation (gratitude)

❑ この程度のことしかできないが、まあ「気は心」と思ってくれ。

Kono teido no koto shika dekinai ga, mā "ki wa kokoro" to omotte kure.

I couldn't get you anything really nice, but I just wanted you to know that my heart's in the right place.

❑ つまらないものですが、「気は心」で、どうぞお受け取りください。

Tsumaranai mono desu ga, "ki wa kokoro" de, dōzo ouketori kudasai.

[It's really nothing, but] I hope you'll accept this small token of my appreciation.

Used when giving a gift to convey the idea that while the gift or amount of money may be small, the thought behind it is sincere.

☞ *kimochi* 気持ち (#2)

kihin 気品 *ki* quality

■ dignity, refinement

❒ このホテルのロビーは格調が高く、調度品にも気品が漂っている。

Kono hoteru no robī wa kakuchō ga takaku, chōdo-hin ni mo kihin ga tadayotte iru.

The lobby of this hotel is a study in elegance, right down to the finely appointed furnishings.

❒ 気品のある顔立ちの老婦人が入って来た。

Kihin no aru kaodachi no rōfujin ga haitte kita.

An elderly matron (of dignified mien) entered.

❒ 新人作家だが、気品のある文章を書く。

Shinjin-sakka da ga, kihin no aru bunshō o kaku.

Though she's a new author, her writing is elegant.

❒ 豪華な中にも気品に満ちたウエディングドレスでございます。

Gōka na naka ni mo kihin ni michita uedingu-doresu de gozaimasu.

It is truely a magnificent and yet throughly refined wedding gown, ma'am.

kibun 気分 *ki* portion

■ feeling(s), mood, the way *one* feels

❒ 気分はどう？

Kibun wa dō?

How do you feel? / How are you doing (feeling)?

❒ 要は気分の問題だ。

Yō wa kibun no mondai da.

Just depends how you look at it (feel about it).

❒ 好きでもない人から交際を申し込まれて複雑な気分だ。

Suki de mo nai hito kara kōsai o mōshikomarete fukuzatsu na kibun da.

I've got mixed feelings about being asked out by someone I'm not really interested in.

❒ とても旅をしたい気分じゃないのよ、いまは。

Totemo tabi o shitai kibun ja nai no yo, ima wa.

Right now I'm in no mood to take a trip.

❒ 土曜の夜じゃね。どうしても勉強する気分にならないもんね。

Doyō no yoru ja ne. Dōshite mo benkyō suru kibun ni naranai mon ne.

Saturday night? Hey, man, no way I can get in the mood to crack the books.

❒ みんな揃いも揃って*アンニュイな気分だった。

Minna soroi mo sorotte annyui no kibun datta.

A feeling (atmosphere) of ennui pervaded the place. / For one and all, the general feeling was one of tedium.

* *soroi mo sorotte*: one and all, every last one

❑ 寝る前にこれを飲めば、気分がさわやかになってよく眠れる。

Neru mae ni kore o nomeba, kibun ga sawayaka ni natte yoku nemureru.

If you take this before you go to bed, you'll feel a whole lot better and sleep soundly.

❑ 高揚した気分が少しは落ち着いてきた。

Kōyō shita kibun ga sukoshi wa ochitsuite kita.

I don't feel quite as worked up as I did before.

❑ 誰も作品をほめなかったので、彼は気分を害したらしい。

Dare mo sakuhin o homenakatta no de, kare wa kibun o gaishita rashii.

I guess his feelings got hurt when no one had anything good to say about his artwork.

❑ タバコは健康に悪いが、気分転換には役立つ。

Tabako wa kenkō ni warui ga, kibun-tenkan ni wa yakudatsu.

Cigarettes may be bad for your health, but they're sure great for a change of pace.

kibun ga ii 気分がいい

1. feel great, feel well

❑ おじいちゃん、今朝は気分がいいですか？

Ojīchan, kesa wa kibun ga ii desu ka?

Are you feeling all right this morning, Grandpa?

❑ 気分がよくなるまでここで安静にしていなさい。

Kibun ga yoku naru made koko de ansei ni shite inasai.

Stay here and rest until you start feeling better.

2. charming, delightful, pleasant

❑ 素直に「はい」と言ってもらえると気分がいい。

Sunao ni "Hai" to itte moraeru to kibun ga ii.

It'd really be nice if she'd simply say, "Yes."

❑ 空気はおいしいし、景色もいいし、ここは本当に気分のいい所だ。

Kūki wa oishii shi, keshiki mo ii shi, koko wa hontō ni kibun no ii tokoro da.

Fresh air, beautiful scenery—this is truly a delightful place.

➡kibun ga warui 気分が悪い

1. feel ill, sick, sick to *one's* stomach; have an upset stomach

❏ 気分が悪い人は手を挙げて申し出てください。

Kibun ga warui hito wa te o agete mōshidete kudasai.

If you're not feeling well, please let me know by raising your hand.

❏ 電車の中で気分が悪くなった。

Densha no naka de kibun ga waruku natta.

I started feeling sick on the train.

❏ 気分が悪くならないうちに乗り物酔いの薬を飲んでおこう。

Kibun ga waruku naranai uchi ni norimono-yoi no kusuri o nonde okō.

Think I'll take some motion sickness medicine before I start feeling sick.

2. sickening, unpleasant

❏ 気分の悪い虐殺場面だったよね。

Kibun no warui gyakusatsu-bamen datta yo ne.

That was one sickening massacre scene, wasn't it.

❏ けんかして以来、あいつの声を聞くだけで気分が悪い。

Kenka shite irai, aitsu no koe o kiku dake de kibun ga warui.

Ever since I had that argument with him, it makes me sick just to hear his voice.

➡kibun-ya 気分屋

■ a moody person, someone who blows hot and cold

❏ 彼みたいな気分屋は客商売には向かないだろう。

Kare mitai na kibun-ya wa kyaku-shōbai ni wa mukanai darō.

I doubt that a moody person like him is suited to dealing with customers.

kimae 気前 front of *ki*

■ generosity, largess, munificence

❏ お前の親父は気前がいいなあ。うちのはケチでだめだ。

Omae no oyaji wa kimae ga ii nā. Uchi no wa kechi de dame da.

Your old man is really generous. Mine's so stingy.

❏ 大山さんっていつも気前よくおごってくれるから大好き。

Koyama-san tte itsumo kimae yoku ogotte kureru kara daisuki.

I really like Koyama, because he always picks up the tab when you go out with him.

Always in conjunction with the adjective *ii* or adverb *yoku*.

---

kimagure 気まぐれ a diversion of *ki*

■ a whim, caprice

❐ 僕の気まぐれにつきあってくれてありがとう。

Boku no kimagure ni tsukiatte kurete arigatō.

Thanks for going along with me on the spur of the moment.

❐ 親父の気まぐれにふりまわされるのはもうご免だ。

Oyaji no kimagure ni furimawasareru no wa mō gomen da.

I'm sick and tired of my dad getting these burrs under his saddle all the time.

❐ あの時のプロポーズは一時の気まぐれだったって言うの？

Ano toki no puropōzu wa ichiji no kimagure datta tte iu no?

So, are you telling me that you proposed to me on a whim, or what?

➡kimagure (na) 気まぐれ(な) *ki* diverted

■ capricious, whimsical, spur-of-the-moment

❐ 彼女の気まぐれな行動には私たちも困っている。

Kanojo no kimagure na kōdō ni wa watashi-tachi mo komatte iru.

Her capricious behavior is giving us a lot of headaches too.

❐ 君も気まぐれな恋人を持って大変だな。

Kimi mo kimagure na koibito o motte taihen da na.

With that fickle girlfriend of yours, I can see life's not easy for you either.

kimazui 気まずい distastful *ki*

■ awkward, ill at ease, sensitive, strained, tense, uncomfortable

❐ 例の件以来、彼と会ってもなんとなく気まずい。

Rei no ken irai, kare to atte mo nan to naku kimazui.

Ever since, there's been a certain awkwardness between us when we meet.

❐ 会議は気まずい雰囲気の中で始まった。

Kaigi wa kimazui fun'iki no naka de hajimatta.

The conference began in an atmosphere of unpleasantness (a constrained atmosphere).

kimama (na) 気まま(な) as *ki* likes

■ willful, selfish; carefree

❐ たまには気ままな一人旅がしてみたいなあ。

Tama ni wa kimama na hitori-tabi ga shite mitai nā.

Once in a while I'd like to just take off on a trip all by myself.

❏ あんまり勝手気ままな人なので誰も相手にしないんだ。

Anmari katte kimama na hito na no de dare mo aite ni shinai n' da.

He's way too full of himself for anybody to take him seriously.

❏ 独身の頃は休日は気ままに過ごせたものだけど、今じゃそういうわけにもいかないね。

Dokushin no koro wa kyūjitsu wa kimama ni sugoseta mono da kedo, ima ja sō iu wake ni mo ikanai ne.

When I was single, I used to be able to do anything I felt like on my days off, but those days are gone now.

⇨ *wagamama (na)* 我がまま(な), *kimakase(na)* 気任せ(な)

kimi 気味 a taste of *ki*

■ a [usually bad, strange, or uncanny] feeling or sensation

❏ いい気味だ。

Ii kimi da.

It serves him (you) right!

❏ いくら作り物と分かっていてもやはり気味が悪い。

Ikura tsukurimono to wakatte ite mo yahari kimi ga warui.

Even though you know it's not real, it still gives you the creeps.

❏ 二十歳の男がそんなに品行方正だったらかえって気味が悪いよ。

Hatachi no otoko ga sonna ni hinkō-hōsei dattara kaette kimi ga warui yo.

On the contrary, for a twenty-year-old to be that well behaved is kind of weird. / There's something eerie about a twenty-year-old guy who's that polite.

❏ なんだか薄気味悪い客だったねえ。

Nandaka usu-kimi-warui kyaku datta nē.

He was kind of a creepy customer (client), wasn't he?

❏ あの家は殺人事件以来空き家で、誰も気味悪がって近づかない。

Ano ie wa satsujin-jiken irai akiya de, dare mo kimi-warugatte chika-zukanai.

That house has been vacant ever since somebody got murdered there, and everybody's so spooked that no one will go near the place.

Although there are idioms in which the word appears to have a positive meaning—*ii kimi da*, or less commonly *kimi ga ii*—both express a feeling of satisfaction upon learning that someone disliked has suffered disappointment or failure and finally gotten what he or she deserves. In practice, *kimi* is found almost exclusively in negative expressions such as *kimi ga warui* and its variant *kimi no warui* or the derivative *kimi-warui*.

⇨ *bukimi (na)* 不気味(な)

-gimi 〜気味 [following a noun] a taste of *ki*

■ a dash, a hint of, a little, somewhat; a touch; a tendency to be ~ , on the ~ side

❏ 今日は風邪気味なのでお先に失礼します。
Kyō wa kaze-gimi na no de osaki ni shitsurei shimasu.
I feel like I'm coming down with a cold, so I think I'll call it a day.

❏ 最近太り気味で服がきつくなってきた。
Saikin futori-gimi de fuku ga kitsuku natte kita.
My clothes are too tight now 'cause I've put on a little weight lately.

❏ 息子はこのごろ怠け気味で、成績が下がってきちゃったのよ。
Musuko wa kono goro namake-gimi de, seiseki ga sagatte kichatta no yo.
My son's gotten rather lazy recently, and his grades are beginning to show it.

❏ おばあちゃんがちょっとボケ気味で心配してるんです。
Obāchan ga chotto boke-gimi de shinpai shite 'ru n' desu.
We're concerned that Grandma might be getting a little senile.

➡kokimi-yoi 小気味よい a little taste of *ki* is good

■ clever, sharp, smart; delightful, happy

❏ 彼女の口からは小気味よいせりふがポンポン出てきた。
Kanojo no kuchi kara wa kokimi-yoi serifu ga ponpon dete kita.
She was spouting off all kinds of witty things.

❏ お宅の自慢料理に小気味よいアクセントをつけるスパイスはいかがですか。
Otaku no jiman-ryōri ni kokimi-yoi akusento o tsukeru supaisu wa ikaga desu ka.
Wouldn't you like to try one of our spices on that special dish of yours for that extra-special little something? [a line that might be heard in a department stores food section]

There is a *kokimi (ga) warui* 小気味(が)悪い, but it's not very common and it's not an antonym of *kokimi-yoi*. It means, "a little creepy," or "kind of weird" and is less common than *usukimi ga warui*, which is exemplified above.

kimuzukashii 気難しい difficult *ki*

■ hard to get along with, cross-grained, difficult, fussy, touchy

❒ 家の父は気難しいから母はいつも腫れ物にさわるようにしてる。

Uchi no chichi wa kimuzukashii kara haha wa itsumo haremono ni sawaru yō ni shite 'ru.

My dad's such a grouch that Mom's got to tiptoe around him.

❒ いつもニコニコしていらしてそんな気難しい方のようには見えないけどねえ。

Itsumo nikoniko shite irashite sonna kimuzukashii kata no yō ni wa mienai kedo nē.

He sure doesn't look like he's that hard to please, the way he always has a smile on his face.

ki mo shiranai de 気も知らないで without even knowing *ki*

■ could(n't) care less about how *someone* feels

❒ 人の気も知らないで呑気なものだ。

Hito no ki mo shiranai de nonki na mono da.

You're one happy-go-lucky gal. Couldn't care less about my feelings, could you.

❒ 親の気も知らないで娘は二人とも好き勝手をしています。

Oya no ki mo shiranai de musume wa futari tomo suki-katte o shite imasu.

Neither of our daughters give so much as a thought to how we feel, they're both so self-centered.

❒ 隣の息子は親の気も知らないで高校をやめてしまった。

Tonari no musuko wa oya no ki mo shiranai de kōkō o yamete shimatta.

Our neighbor's son up and quit high school without a thought for his parents' feelings.

The *hito no ki* and *oya no ki* seen in the first two example sentences above, while literally meaning "a person's *ki*" and "a parent's *ki*" respectively refer in fact to that of the speaker, and in this way are similar to saying that someone could care less "about how other people feel," when a native speaker of English understands that it is the speaker's feelings that are being hurt.

---

ki mo sozoro 気もそぞろ *ki* is restless

■ can't keep *one's* mind on, have trouble concentrating on

❒ 彼女朝から気もそぞろで間違えてばかりいるよ。

Kanojo asa kara ki mo sozoro de machigaete bakari iru yo.

She's been distracted since morning and making a lot of mistakes.

❒ 今は気もそぞろだから何を言っても無口だと思うな。

Ima wa ki mo sozoro da kara nani o itte mo muda da to omou na.

It won't do you any good to talk to her now; her mind's someplace else.

⟶ *kokoro mo sozoro* 心もそぞろ

kimochi 気持ち *ki* holding

1. feelings, the way one feels

❒ まだ気持ちの整理がつかないんだろう。

Mada kimochi no seiri ga tsukanai n' darō.

I don't think she's sorted out her feelings about it yet. / I think she still has mixed feelings about it.

❒ お気持ちはよく分かりますとも。

Okimochi wa yoku wakarimasu tomo.

I know exactly how you feel.

❒ 後は君の気持ち次第だよ。

Ato wa kimi no kimochi shidai da yo.

It's up to you from here on out.

❒ あなたならこんな時どんな気持ちがする？

Anata nara konna toki donna kimochi ga suru?

How would you feel (What would you think) if you were in my place?

❒ 今はまだあの人を許す気持ちにはなれないわ。

Ima wa mada ano hito o yurusu kimochi ni wa narenai wa.

I still can't (I'm still not ready to) forgive him.

❒ 張りつめていた気持ちが彼の一言で一度に楽になりましたよ。

Haritsumete ita kimochi ga kare no hitokoto de ichido ni raku ni nari-mashita yo.

All the tension I had been feeling just melted away when he spoke to me.

❒ からだの心配より「休んではいけない」という気持ちの方が強かった。

Karada no shinpai yori "Yasunde wa ikenai" to iu kimochi no hō ga tsu-yokatta.

I was more concerned about missing work than I was about my health.

❏ ああ、いい気持ちだった。やっぱり温泉はいいなあ。

Ā, ii kimochi datta. Yappari onsen wa ii nā.

Oh, man, that felt great! There's nothing like a hot spring.

➡kimochi (ga) ii 気持ち(が)いい the way *ki* is held is good

■ feel good, feel great

1. (of a person's or animal's pleasant sensation) feel good

❏ 早起きすると気持ちがいいなあ。

Hayaoki suru to kimochi ga ii nā.

It feels so good to get up early.

❏ タマのやつ気持ちよさそうに日溜まりに寝そべってるよ。

Tama no yatsu kimochi yosasō ni hidamari ni nesobette 'ru yo.

Tama [the cat] is napping happily in the sunlight.

2. (of a thing) pleasant, pleasing

❏ 気持ちのいい朝だなあ。

Kimochi no ii asa da nā.

What a wonderful morning! / A morning like this makes you happy to be alive.

❏ さっぱりした気持ちのいい人ですよ。

Sappari shita kimochi no ii hito desu yo.

He's a very refreshing person to be around.

➡kimochi (ga) warui 気持ち(が)悪い the way *ki* is held is bad

1. (of a person's or animal's unpleasant sensation) feel bad

❏ 気持ちが悪いんだったら、この薬をお飲みなさい。

Kimochi ga warui n' dattara, kono kusuri o onominasai.

Take this medicine if you don't feel well (if you're feeling under the weather).

❏ 靴がビショビショで、気持ち悪いよ。

Kutsu ga bishobisho de, kimochi warui yo.

These shoes are soaking wet. They feel terrible.

❏ 飲み過ぎて気持ち悪くなっても知らないぞ。

Nomisugite kimochi waruku natte mo shiranai zo.

Don't come crying to me if you drink too much and get sick.

2. (of a thing) disagreeable, disgusting, unpleasant

❏ 彼女があんまり機嫌がいいと気持ちが悪いね。

Kanojo ga anmari kigen ga ii to kimochi ga warui ne.

It gives you the creeps when she gets in such a good mood.

❏ 気持ちの悪い絵にしか見えないけど、これが傑作なの？

Kimochi no warui e ni shika mienai kedo, kore ga kessaku na no?

I don't see anything except a disgusting painting. How can this be a "masterpiece"?

2. a (small) token of *one's* appreciation

❒ ささやかですが、私どもの気持ちでございます。
Sasayaka desu ga, watakushi-domo no kimochi de gozaimasu.
This is a mere token of our gratitude.

❒ ほんの気持ちばかりですが、どうぞお納めください。
Hon no kimochi bakari desu ga, dōzo oosame kudasai.
I hope you will accept this small gift as a token of my appreciation.
  ☞ *ki wa kokoro* 気は心

3. a bit, hair, tad

❒ 裾を気持ち短くしてもらいたいんですが。
Suso o kimochi mijikaku shite moraitai n' desu ga.
I'd like to have the hem raised just a smidgen.

❒ その絵、気持ち上にずらした方がいいんじゃないの。
Sono e, kimochi ue ni zurashita hō ga ii n' ja nai no.
Wouldn't that picture be better just a shade higher?
  ⇨ *kokoromochi* 心持ち

kiyasui 気安い easy *ki*

■ relaxed, familiar, friendly

❒ 気安い友人が何人もいて、俺は本当に幸せ者だ。
Kiyasui yūjin ga nannin mo ite, ore wa hontō ni shiawasemono da.
I'm a lucky guy to have so many friends I feel comfortable around.

❒ あの先生には気安く何でも話せるってみんな言ってるよ。
Ano sensei ni wa kiyasuku nan de mo hanaseru tte minna itte 'ru yo.
Everyone says that that professor is very approachable (easy to talk to).

❒ 困ったことができたらいつでも気安く相談に来たまえ。
Komatta koto ga dekitara itsu de mo kiyasuku sōdan ni kitamae.
Any time you have a problem, feel free to come and talk it over.

❒ あんな気安い言い方をされると不愉快だ。
Anna kiyasui iikata o sareru to fu-yukai da.
It's not very pleasant to be spoken to so offhandedly.

❒ 気安くあだ名を呼ばないでくださいな。
Kiyasuku adana o yobanai de kudasai na.
Don't get so familiar that you're going around calling me by my nickname.
  ☞ *ki ga okenai* 気がおけない, *kigaru (na)* 気軽(な) (see under *ki ga karui* 気が軽い), *kiraku (na)* 気楽(な) (see under *ki ga raku ni naru* 気が楽になる)

⇨ *kokoroyasui* 心安い

☛ *kigane suru* 気兼ねする (see under *kigane* 気兼ね)

kiryoku 気力 power of *ki*

■ drive, energy, heart, inner strength, mettle, (emotional) staying power, vitality, willpower

❒ このプロジェクトには、気力、体力、知力のすべてが要求されている。

Kono purojekuto ni wa, kiryoku, tairyoku, chiryoku no subete ga yōkyū sarete iru.

Energy, intelligence and stamina are all required for this project.

❒ 生き続けようという気力を失った。

Ikitsuzukeyō to iu kiryoku o ushinatta.

She lost the will to live.

❒ 彼の場合は気力だけで持ちこたえたようなものだ。

Kare no bāi wa kiryoku dake de mochikotaeta yō na mono da.

He hung on almost by sheer intestinal fortitude.

ki o ireru 気を入れる put *one's ki* into

■ get into doing something, get enthusiastic about something

❒ 好きでもないことに気を入れるのは実に難しい。

Suki de mo nai koto ni ki o ireru no wa jitsu ni muzukashii.

It's really hard to get into doing something that you don't like.

❒ もっと気を入れて勉強しないと、いつまでたっても試験には受からないよ。

Motto ki o irete benkyō shinai to, itsu made tatte mo shiken ni wa ukaranai yo.

If you don't buckle down and study, you're never going to pass the test.

Compared to *ki ga hairu*, *ki o ireru* implies that conscious effort is involved.

☞ *ki ga hairu* 気が入る

ki o ushinau 気を失う lose *ki*

■ black out, faint, go out like a light, lose consciousness, pass out, slip into unconsciousness (darkness)

❑ ボクシングではスパーリング中に打たれて気を失うことも珍しくない。

Bokushingu de wa supāringu-chū ni utarete ki o ushinau koto mo mezurashiku nai.

In boxing it's not all that uncommon to get knocked out when you're just sparring.

❑ 大統領は即死だったが夫人は気を失っただけで無事だった。

Daitōryō wa sokushi datta ga fujin wa ki o ushinatta dake de buji datta.

The president died instantly, but his wife just fainted and emerged unscathed.

Entails a complete loss of consciousness, unlike *ki ga tōku naru* which usually means *feeling* faint.

☞ *ki ga tōku naru* 気が遠くなる(#1), *kizetsu suru* 気絶する
⇨ *shisshin suru* 失神する
☛ *ki ga tsuku* 気がつく (#3)

ki o ochitsukeru 気を落ち着ける calm *ki* down

■ calm *oneself* down, regain *one's* composure, settle down

❑ 大失敗の後、気を落ち着ける間もなく次の仕事にかからねばならなかった。

Daishippai no ato, ki o ochitsukeru ma mo naku tsugi no shigoto ni kakaraneba naranakatta.

Right after this major screw-up I had to pull myself together and start right in on another job.

❑ 気を落ちつけて最初からもう一度話して下さい。

Ki o ochitsukete saisho kara mō ichido hanashite kudasai.

Now calm down and start again from the beginning.

also *ki o ochitsukaseru* 気を落ち着かせる
☞ *ki o shizumeru* 気を静める

ki o otosu 気を落とす drop *ki*

■ be (become) dejected, depressed, despondent, disheartened, downcast

❑ よくあることだから、気を落とすことはないさ。

Yoku aru koto da kara, ki o otosu koto wa nai sa.

It could happen to anybody, don't let it get you down. / Happens all the time, man. Don't sweat it.

❐ 南田さんは3年もつきあっていた彼女にふられて気を落としている。

Minamida-san wa sannen mo tsukiatte ita kanojo ni furarete ki o otoshite iru.

Minamida's bummed out 'cause this gal he'd been going out with for three years dumped him.

❐ 気を落とさないで。またいいこともあるよ。

Ki o otosanaide. Mata ii koto mo aru yo.

Don't get so discouraged. Things will start looking up before long.

➡kiochi suru 気落ちする be dropped *ki*

■ be discouraged, despondent; feel low; lose heart

❐ 北山君は今年も試験に受からなかったのですっかり気落ちしている。

Kitayama-kun wa kotoshi mo shiken ni ukaranakatta no de sukkari kiochi shite iru.

Kitayama's down in the dumps 'cause he failed the exam again this year.

❐ 気落ちした父を慰めようと、姉夫婦が子供を連れて遊びに来た。

Kiochi shita chichi o nagusameyō to, ane-fūfu ga kodomo o tsurete asobi ni kita.

My sister and her husband came over with their kids to cheer Dad up.

ki o kubaru 気を配る distribute *ki*

■ pay attention to, take care (to), be careful (to), take pains (to)

❐ もう少し身だしなみに気を配るようにしたらどうだい？

Mō sukoshi midashinami ni ki o kubaru yō ni shitara dō dai?

Don't you think you ought to pay a little more attention to your appearance?

❐ 平等になるように気を配ったが、それでも一部の人から苦情が出た。

Byōdō ni naru yō ni ki o kubatta ga, sore de mo ichibu no hito kara kujō ga deta.

I was careful to arrange things equitably, but there were still complaints from some people.

❐ 出発日によって航空運賃が違うから、スケジュールの調整には気を配るべきだ。

Shuppatsu-bi ni yotte kōkū-unchin ga chigau kara, sukejūru no chōsei ni wa ki o kubaru beki da.

KI O KUBARU 109

You should take care when deciding your itinerary because airline ticket prices vary depending on the date of departure.

See note at *kizukau* 気遣う for explanation of differences among this entry, *kizukau*, and *ki o tsukau* 気を使う.

☞ ki o tsukau 気を使う

➡kikubari 気配り doling out *ki*

■ attention, care, pains

❒ 道子さんのさりげない気配りが嬉しかったのよ。

Michiko-san no sarigenai kikubari ga ureshikatta no yo.

The way Michiko was so attentive without being obtrusive was really nice.

❒ いくら若いからと言っても、もう少し気配りをするべきだ。

Ikura wakai kara to itte mo, mō sukoshi kikubari o suru beki da.

Sure he's young and all, but just the same he's got to pay more attention to how his actions affect other people.

❒ 気配りが足りなくて、不愉快な思いをさせてしまった。

Kikubari ga tarinakute, fu-yukai na omoi o sasete shimatta.

I'm afraid I was a little tactless and ended up offending him.

❒ 岡田さんはいつもまわりを大事にする典型的な気配りの人だ。

Okada-san wa itsumo mawari o daiji ni suru tenkei-teki na kikubari no hito da.

Mr. Okada is a typical caring person, always seeing to the needs of those around him.

❒ 細かい気配りが行き届いたすばらしいパーティーだったね。

Komakai kikubari ga yukitodoita subarashii pātī datta ne.

That was one great party, wasn't it. The preparations were so thoroughgoing.

Contrasted to *kizukai*, which describes the care for others that arises naturally from a gentle, caring person, *kikubari* describes more the artifice or technique necessary, particularly in Japanese society, to insure that human relations remain congenial and work gets done. So while *kizukai* is greatly appreciated, some degree of *kikubari* is expected, indeed demanded, from adults in Japan. It should not, by the way, be confused with 気配 *kehai*.

☞ *kizukai* 気遣い (see under *kizukau* 気遣う), *ki o tsukau* 気を使う
⇨ *hairyo* 配慮, *kokoro-kubari* 心配り

ki o shizumeru 気を静める quiet *ki* down

■ calm down, get a grip (on *oneself*), get hold of *oneself*, settle down

❒ 気を静めてよく聞いてほしいんだ。
Ki o shizumete yoku kiite hoshii n' da.
Simmer down now and listen.

❒ まずはこれでも飲んで気を静めることだ。
Mazu wa kore de mo nonde ki o shizumeru koto da.
The first thing you've got to do is take (drink) this and try to calm yourself down.
    ☞ *ki o ochitsukeru* 気を落ち着ける

➡ki ga shizumaru 気が静まる *ki* quiets down

■ calm down, regain *one's* composure, settle down

❒ 彼の気が静まるのを待ってもう一度話してみよう。
Kare no ki ga shizumaru no o matte mō ichido hanashite miyō.
I think I'll give him a chance to settle down before I talk to him again.

❒ ようやく気が静まったらしい。
Yōyaku ki ga shizumatta rashii.
Looks like she's finally cooled off.
    ☞ *ki ga ochitsuku* 気が落ち着く
    ☞ *ki ga tatsu* 気が立つ

ki o sogu 気をそぐ shave off *ki*

■ dampen, dishearten, throw cold water on, throw a wet blanket on

❒ せっかくやる気になってるのに気をそぐようなこと言うもんじゃないよ。
Sekkaku yaru ki ni natte 'ru no ni ki o sogu yō na koto iu mon ja nai yo.
Why are you trying to discourage him just when he's getting into it?

❒ あの人の一言ですっかり気をそがれてしまった。
Ano hito no hitokoto de sukkari ki o sogarete shimatta.
One word from him was all it took to put a damper on my enthusiasm.

ki o sorasu 気を逸らす divert *ki*

1. let *one's* mind wander, lose concentration, stop paying attention, woolgather

❏ 機械での作業中に気を逸らすのは事故につながる。

Kikai de no sagyō-chū ni ki o sorasu no wa jiko ni tsunagaru.

If you let yourself get distracted when you're operating machinery, it could lead to an accident.

❏ 気を逸らさないでちゃんと聞きなさい。

Ki o sorasanai de chanto kikinasai.

Quit fooling around and pay attention.

2. break *someone's* concentration, distract, divert *someone's* attention, get *someone's* attention

❏ 俺がサツの気を逸らすから、その間にお前は裏口へ回れ。

Ore ga satsu no ki o sorasu kara, sono aida ni omae wa uraguchi e maware.

While I'm distracting the cop, you go around to the back.

❏ 先生の気を宿題から逸らそうとして皆で次々に質問した。

Sensei no ki o shukudai kara sorasō to shite minna de tsugi-tsugi ni shitsumon shita.

Everyone was asking all kinds of questions, trying to make the teacher forget about the homework assignment.

➡ki ga soreru 気が逸れる *ki is distracted*

■ get distracted, stop paying attention

❏ どんなにおもしろい講義でもやはりときどき気が逸れる。

Donna ni omoshiroi kōgi de mo yahari tokidoki ki ga soreru.

No matter how interesting a lecture is, your mind wanders now and then.

❏ ふと気が逸れた瞬間に包丁で指を切ってしまった。

Futo ki ga soreta shunkan ni hōchō de yubi o kitte shimatta.

I cut my finger with the kitchen knife the second I stopped paying attention to what I was doing.

☞ *ki ga chiru* 気が散る

ki o tsukau 気を使う *use ki*

1. [of people] look after, take (good) care of, take pains

❏ 添乗員というのは気を使うわりに感謝されない仕事だよ。

Tenjō-in to iu no wa ki o tsukau wari ni kansha sarenai shigoto da yo.

For all the pains they take, tour conductors don't get much respect. / Being a tour conductor is a thankless job that requires a lot of pains-taking work.

❏ どうぞもう気を使わないでください。

Dōzo mō ki o tsukawanai de kudasai.

Don't worry about me. / Don't mind me.

❏ あまり気を使われるとかえって窮屈な思いをする。

Amari ki o tsukawareru to kaette kyūkutsu na omoi o suru.

It's actually an imposition when someone's always fussing over you.

❏ へんに気を使わずに遠慮なく言ってもらった方がいい。

Hen ni ki o tsukawazu ni enryo naku itte moratta hō ga ii.

Why don't you tell me what you think without worrying how I'm going to feel about it (take it).

2. [of things or events] pay attention to, be uppermost in *one's* thoughts

❏ どの都市も水源地の環境保全にはかなり気を使っている。

Dono toshi mo suigen-chi no kankyō-hozen ni wa kanari ki o tsukatte iru.

Urban areas all over are paying close attention to the protection of their watersheds.

❏ 営業でよく外を歩くので、靴には人一倍気を使う。

Eigyō de yoku soto o aruku no de, kutsu ni wa hito-ichibai ki o tsukau.

I'm pounding the pavement all the time on my sales route, so I pay a lot more attention to my shoes than most people do.

❏ 食事にも気を使い、自然食品を買うようにしている。

Shokuji ni mo ki o tsukai, shizen-shokuhin o kau yō ni shite iru.

I also watch what I eat and try to buy natural foods when I can.

❏ アメリカ人が健康に気を使い出して20年もたっています。

Amerika-jin ga kenkō ni ki o tsukaidashite nijū-nen mo tatte imasu.

Twenty years have already passed since Americans first began to pay attention to their health.

❏ 細かいところにまで気を使ったデザインですよね。

Komakai tokoro ni made ki o tsukatta dezain desu yo ne.

They sure have paid close attention to detail in this design.

See the note at *kizukau* 気遣う for the differences among this entry, *kizukau*, and *ki o kubaru* 気を配る.

☞ *ki o kubaru* 気を配る, *kizukau* 気遣う, *kigane (o) suru* 気兼ね(を)する (under *kigane*)

ki o tsukeru 気をつける put *ki* on

■ be attentive (to), be careful, take note of, take care (of)

❏ 気をつけて。

Ki o tsukete.

Be careful. / Take care. / Have a good time. [A common expression when parting company.]

❒ 今回は見逃すが、この次からよく気をつけるようにしなさい。

Konkai wa minogasu ga, kono tsugi kara yoku ki o tsukeru yō ni shinasai.

I'm going to overlook (I'm not going to make an issue of) it this time, but you'd better be a little more careful from now on.

❒ 夜はまだ冷えますから、どうぞお体にはお気をつけて。

Yoru wa mada hiemasu kara, dōzo okarada ni wa oki o tsukete.

The nights still get chilly, so take good care of yourself. [A typical ending for a letter written in early spring.]

❒ 気をつけてよく見ると小さい虫がたくさん葉の裏にいた。

Ki o tsukete yoku miru to chiisai mushi ga takusan ha no ura ni ita.

If you look really carefully, you can see all kinds of tiny insects on the underside of the leaf.

❒ これからの季節に気をつけたいのが食中毒だ。

Kore kara no kisetsu ni ki o tsuketai no ga shoku-chūdoku da.

One thing you want to watch out for this time of year is food poisoning.

❒ 痛い！　気をつけろよ。あぶないなあ。

Itai! Ki o tsukero yo. Abunai nā.

Ouch! Watch it, huh. You're going to hurt somebody.

By the way, The Japanese military equivalent of the English "Attention!" is *"Ki o tsuke!"*

☞ *ki o kubaru* 気を配る

ki o torareru　気を取られる　have one's *ki* taken

■ *one's* mind is taken off *something,* get distracted

❒ 運転中に窓の外に気を取られると危険だよ。

Unten-chū ni mado no soto ni ki o torareru to kiken da yo.

Don't let yourself get distracted while you're driving. It's dangerous.

❒ 派手な喧嘩に気を取られているうちに財布をすられたらしいんです。

Hade na kenka ni ki o torarete iru uchi ni saifu o surareta rashii n' desu.

I guess I must have had my pocket picked while my attention was diverted by a loud argument.

❒ 前の席の美人に気を取られて、講義が耳に入らなかった。

Mae no seki no bijin ni ki o torarete, kōgi ga mimi ni hairanakatta.

I got distracted by this raving beauty sitting in front of me in class and didn't hear a thing the prof said.

For what it's worth, the result of having your *ki* "taken" (*ki o torareru*) is that your *ki* "disperses" (*ki ga chiru*). Want more? See the entry for *ki ga chiru*.

---

ki o torinaosu 気を取り直す grab hold of *ki* again

■ buck up, collect *oneself*, collect *one's* thoughts, pull *oneself* together, regroup

❒ 今は先のことを心配するよりまず気を取り直すことだ。
Ima wa saki no koto o shinpai suru yori mazu ki o torinaosu koto da.
Right now it's more important for you to pull yourself together than worry about the future.

❒ 人生これからなんだから、気を取り直して頑張れよ。
Jinsei kore kara nan da kara, ki o torinaoshite ganbare yo.
Look, you've got your whole life ahead of you, so just pull yourself together and keep plugging away.

❒ 西村さんは少し気を取り直したらしく、笑顔も見せるようになった。
Nishimura-san wa sukoshi ki o torinaoshita rashiku, egao mo miseru yō ni natta.
Nishimura seems to have perked up a bit and has even started to smile.

ki o nomareru 気を呑まれる have one's *ki* swallowed

■ be overpowered; be set back on *one's* heels, be taken aback

❒ 会場の熱気にすっかり気を呑まれてしまった。
Kaijō no nekki ni sukkari ki o nomarete shimatta.
I was overcome by the excitement that swept the place.

❒ 最初から最後まで気を呑まれっぱなしだったよ。
Saisho kara saigo made ki o nomareppanashi datta yo.
I was simply overwhelmed from beginning to end.

ki o haku 気を吐く spit *ki* out

■ [of speech] talk up a storm; [of behavior] do a good job, outdo *oneself*, put on a good show, work out

❑ 中山さんは自信満々で盛んに気を吐いている。
Nakayama-san wa jishin-manman de sakan ni ki o haite iru.
Nakayama's brimming with confidence and going all out.

❑ 同窓会では旧友と大いに気を吐き合った。
Dōsō-kai de wa kyūyū to ōi ni ki o hakiatta.
I talked up a storm with an old friend at the reunion.

ki o haru 気を張る   stretch *ki* out

■ be ready (for anything), be on *one's* guard, be on the lookout for

❑ そんなに気を張らなくても大丈夫だよ。
Sonna ni ki o haranakute mo daijōbu da yo.
You don't have to be so uptight.

❑ 試合中は気を張ってるから寒さなんか感じないのさ。
Shiai-chū wa ki o hatte 'ru kara samusa nanka kanjinai no sa.
I'm so focused during a game that a little cold doesn't even register.

ki o haritsumeru 気を張りつめる   to draw *ki* taut

■ be on edge, on *one's* toes; be tense, under a strain, under a lot of pressure

❑ 受験生たちはみんな気を張りつめた表情で教室へ向かった。
Jukensei-tachi wa minna ki o haritsumeta hyōjō de kyōshitsu e mukatta.
All those taking the test headed for the classroom with tenses looks on their faces.

❑ 朝から気を張りつめていて、すっかり肩がこっちゃったよ。
Asa kara ki o haritsumete ite, sukkari kata ga kotchatta yo.
I've been under such a strain since morning that now I've got a stiff neck.

Ki o haritsumeru describes a more intense form of concentration or tension than *ki o haru*.

☞ *ki ga haru* 気が張る
⇨ *kibaru* 気張る, *ganbaru* 頑張る
☛ *ki ga yasumaru* 気が休まる

ki o hiku 気を引く pull *ki*

■ get *someone* to notice (pay attention to) *one*, sound (feel) *someone* out (about how he or she feels about oneself)

❏ 彼はしきりと私の気を引くような素振りを見せているのよ。
Kare wa shikiri to watashi no ki o hiku yō na soburi o misete iru no yo.
He's doing his best to attract my attention.

❏ あの人の気を引こうとしていろいろ試してみたが、全く反応がない。
Ano hito no ki o hikō to shite iroiro tameshite mita ga, mattaku hannō ga nai.
I've tried everything I can think of to get him to notice me, but there's been absolutely no reaction.

Used of someone trying indirectly to gain the attention and affection of the opposite sex, it has nothing to do with whistling or waving arms.

⇨ *kokoro o hiku* 心を引く

ki o mawasu 気を回す rotate *one's ki*

■ be mistrustful, (overly) suspicious, suspecting, uptight; get the wrong idea, take *something* (*someone*) wrong

❏ そこまで気を回す必要はない。
Soko made ki o mawasu hitsuyō wa nai.
I think you're reading too much into the situation.

❏ 君は気を回し過ぎるよ。
Kimi wa ki o mawashisugiru yo.
You try to read between the lines too much. / You think too much.

Not to be confused with its cognate *ki ga mawaru* 気が回る, which means to be thoughtful or considerate. *Ki o mawasu* is used critically of one who is thought to be either too suspicious, always looking for the ulterior motive which doesn't exist, or worrying needlessly about insignificant things.

---

ki o motaseru 気を持たせる give someone *ki* to hold

■ get *someone's* hopes up, raise *someone's* expectations

❏ 気を持たせられてさ、脈がある*と思ったのが甘かった。

Ki o motaserarete sa, myaku ga aru to omotta no ga amakatta.

The way she got my hopes up, I thought I had a chance. Guess it was wishful thinking.

> * *myaku ga aru*: lit., have a pulse; fig., have a future. When used of relations between the sexes, indicates a hope that one may gain the favor of another.

❏ さんざん気を持たせておきながら土壇場で逃げてしまった。

Sanzan ki o motasete okinagara dotanba de nigete shimatta.

He led me on, then dumped me at the last minute.

ki o ~ motsu 気を~持つ hold *one's ki* (in some way)

In general, the following expressions are used when advising someone or describing the attitude of a person who is preparing to deal with a difficult situation. An adverb, the *-ku* form of an *-i* adjective, or the *ni* form of a *na* adjective appears in the ellipsis. With the exception of *ki o shikkari motsu*, the idioms that follow are each related to another similar expression included in this book. The differences between them and *ki ga tashika (na)*, *ki ga tsuyoi*, *ki ga nagai*, and *ki ga raku (na)* are as follows.

The distinction between *ki ga tsuyoi* and *ki o tsuyoku motsu* is representative of the others. While the former is used of those perceived to be more tenacious or stubborn than normal, and thus describes an uncommon personality trait, the latter is an admonition not to waver or weaken in the face of some disasterous or trying situation—not, in other words, to become fainthearted or *ki ga yowai*, the opposite of *ki ga tsuyoi*. A person who is described as *ki o tsuyoku motte iru,* therefore, is not necessarily particularly strong-willed. Similarly, *kiraku na* describes a laid-back personality and *ki o raku ni shite* a relatively relaxed situation while *ki o raku ni motte* encourages someone who has already tensed up not to do so, or at least to remain as unpreturbed as possible.

For more information about the specific idioms below, see the expressions indicated after each entry.

➡ki o shikkari motsu 気をしっかり持つ hold *ki* firmly

■ be brave, be strong, brace up, buck up, hang tough

❏ 傷は浅いですよ。気をしっかり持ちなさい。

Kizu wa asai desu yo. Ki o shikkari mochinasai.

It's a shallow wound. Hang in there.

❏ 気をしっかり持って聞いて下さい。残念なお知らせです。

Ki o shikkari motte kiite kudasai. Zannen na oshirase desu.

You've got to be brave now. I've got some bad news.

Used to urge someone not to give in to pain, not to lose consciousness.
No similar expression using *ki*.

---

ki o tashika ni motsu 気を確かに持つ hold *ki* certainly

■ brace up, hang on, hold on, ready *oneself*, summon *one's* courage

❑ 母さん、気を確かに持ってくれ。父さんの病気はもう手遅れだそうだ。

Kāsan, ki o tashika ni motte kure. Tōsan no byōki wa mō te-okure da sō da.

Brace yourself, Mom. They say there's nothing they can do now for Dad.

❑ 取り乱すんじゃない。気を確かに持つんだ。

Torimidasu n' ja nai. Ki o tashika ni motsu n' da.

Don't go to pieces on me now. Get hold of yourself.

    ☞ *ki ga tashika (na)* 気が確か(な), *shōki* 正気

➡ki o tsuyoku motsu 気を強く持つ hold *ki* strongly

■ keep the faith, be resolute, be steadfast, be strong, be unwavering

❑ 子供たちのためにもあなたが気を強く持って頑張って下さい。

Kodomo-tachi no tame ni mo anata ga ki o tsuyoku motte ganbatte kudasai.

For the children's sake too, you must be strong.

❑ こんなことぐらいでへこたれないで、気を強く持とうよ。

Konna koto gurai de hekotarenai de, ki o tsuyoku motō yo.

Hey, don't let something like this get you down. Pull yourself together.

    ☞ *ki ga tsuyoi* 気が強い

➡ki o nagaku motsu 気を長く持つ hold *ki* for a long time

■ be patient, persevere, stick to *something*

❑ 外国との合弁事業の成功には気を長く持つことが必要です。

Gaikoku to no gōben-jigyō no seikō ni wa ki o nagaku motsu koto ga hitsuyō desu.

Making a go of an international joint venture requires patience (a long-term commitment).

❑ 焦って失敗するより、気を長く持ってよい結果を待ちましょう。

Asette shippai suru yori, ki o nagaku motte yoi kekka o machimashō.

Instead of getting impatient, why don't we hang on and see how it turns out.

    ☞ *ki ga nagai* 気が長い

➡ki o raku ni motsu 気を楽に持つ hold *ki* easily

■ calm *oneself,* relax, take it easy

❒ 面接試験では気を楽に持って自分の言葉で話しなさい。

Mensetsu-shiken de wa ki o raku ni motte jibun no kotoba de hanashi-nasai.

When you go for the interview, just relax and speak as you normally do.

❒ 堅くならないで、どうぞ気を楽にお持ち下さい。

Kataku naranai de, dōzo ki o raku ni omochi kudasai.

Try not to tense up; just go ahead and relax.

　　☞ *ki ga raku (na)* 気が楽(な) (see under *ki ga raku ni naru* 気が楽になる)

ki o yurusu 気を許す allow *ki*

1. relax, drop *one's* guard, let *one's* guard down, let up

❒ 男に気を許すなよ。

Otoko ni ki o yurusu na yo.

Don't let your guard down around men. / Keep those guys at arm's length.

❒ 消防署の当直は夜中でも気を許すことは出来ない。

Shōbō-sho no tōchoku wa yonaka de mo ki o yurusu koto wa dekinai.

A fireman on duty can't relax even in the middle of the night.

❒ あの人との交渉では決して気を許してはならない。

Ano hito to no kōshō de wa kesshite ki o yurushite wa naranai.

You have to keep on your toes every minute when you're negotiating with her.

❒ 犯人が気を許した瞬間、警官は彼を取り押さえた。

Hannin ga ki o yurushita shunkan, keikan wa kare o toriosaeta.

The police overpowered the criminal the second he relaxed his guard.

　　☞ *ki ga yurumu* 気が緩む (see under *ki o yurumeru*), *ki o yurumeru* 気を緩める, *ki o nuku* 気を抜く

2. open up to *someone,* let *someone* into *one's* heart

❒ あんな奴に気を許したのが間違いだった。

Anna yatsu ni ki o yurushita no ga machigai datta.

I should have never let a guy like him into my life.

❒ 俊雄さんには気を許して何でも話せる。

Toshio-san ni wa ki o yurushite nan de mo hanaseru.

I can open up to Toshio and tell him everything.

　　⇨ *kokoro o yurusu* 心を許す

ki o yoku suru 気をよくする make *ki* good

■ be buoyed up, encouraged; be in a good mood; flatter *one-self*

❐ 何か気をよくすることがあったらしく朝から機嫌がいい。

Nanika ki o yoku suru koto ga atta rashiku asa kara kigen ga ii.

Something uplifting must have happened to her; she's been in a good mood since morning.

❐ 五回のホームランで気をよくしたタイガースは勢いに乗って楽勝した。

Gokai no hōmuran de ki o yoku shita Taigāsu wa ikioi ni notte rakushō shita.

A fifth-inning home run gave the Tigers a lift that carried them on to victory.

❐ 彼女と一回だけデートしたぐらいで気をよくするもんじゃないぞ。

Kanojo to ikkai dake dēto shita gurai de ki o yoku suru mon ja nai zo.

You went out with her, like, one time? So what!

❐ 思いがけずほめられてすっかり気をよくした。

Omoigakezu homerarete sukkari ki o yoku shita.

I was on cloud nine when she unexpectedly paid me a compliment.

❐ 新製品の大ヒットで、社長はかなり気をよくしている。

Shin-seihin no daihitto de, shachō wa kanari ki o yoku shite iru.

The boss is in seventh heaven since that new product's proved so popular.

　☛ *ki o waruku suru* 気を悪くする

ki o waruku suru 気を悪くする make *ki* bad

■ feel bad; have *one's* feelings hurt, take offense, be offended

❐ あそこまで言えばいくら友だちでも気を悪くするさ。

Asoko made ieba ikura tomodachi de mo ki o waruku suru sa.

I don't care how good a friend he is, when you say something like that it's bound to hurt his feelings.

❐ 気を悪くしたみたいですぐ帰ってしまった。

Ki o waruku shita mitai de sugu kaette shimatta.

She must have been offended (gotten her nose out of joint), the way she up and left.

❐ どうぞお気を悪くなさらないで下さい。

Dōzo oki o waruku nasaranai de kudasai.

Please don't take offense. / Don't take it the wrong way.

⇨ *kibun o waruku suru* 気分を悪くする, *kibun o gaisuru* 気分を害する (both under *kibun* 気分)

☛ *ki o yoku suru* 気をよくする

kyōki 狂気 crazy *ki*

■ insanity, madness

❒ 弁護士は被告人の狂気を理由に無罪を主張した。
Bengo-shi wa hikoku-nin no kyōki o riyū ni muzai o shuchō shita.
The attorney for the accused pleaded not guilty by reason of insanity.

❒ まるで狂気にとりつかれたような仕事ぶりじゃありませんか。
Marude kyōki ni toritsukareta yō na shigoto-buri ja arimasen ka.
You're really working like mad there, aren't you.

❒ 彼の狂気じみた言動には家族も困り果てているらしい。
Kare no kyōki-jimita gendō ni wa kazoku mo komarihatete iru rashii.
I heard his family is just about at its wit's end over his crazy (insane, outlandish) behavior.

☞ *kichigai* 気違い (see under *ki ga chigau* 気が違う)

☛ *shōki* 正気

kuike 食い気 eating *ki*

■ desire (to eat)

❒ 旅行の行き先を決めるのには景色の良さより食い気の方が優先する。
Ryokō no yukisaki o kimeru no ni wa keshiki no yosa yori kuike no hō ga yūsen suru.
I decide where I want to travel based on what the food is like rather than the scenery.

❒ 食い気の塊みたいなやつでさ、いつも2人前食うんだぜ。
Kuike no katamari mitai na yatsu de sa, itsumo ninin-mae kuu n' da ze.
Guy's a bottomless pit, man. Eats enough for two people every time he sits down at the table.

Not to be confused with the notion of appetite—something that can come and go—*kuike* is here to stay, a sort of personality trait. Consequently, there are no *kuike ga aru (nai, suru)* or *kuike o moyōsu (oboeru)* constructions.

☞ *iroke yori kuike* 色気より食い気 (see under *iroke* 色気)

kedakai 気高い high *ki*

■ aristocratic, blue-blooded, noble; exhalted, grand, imposing, regal

❏ 彼女の指には気高いグリーンのエメラルドが輝いていた。

Kanojo no yubi ni wa kedakai gurīn no emerarudo ga kagayaite ita.

A majestic green emerald sparkled from its perch on her finger.

❏ 皇族になられる前からも気高い雰囲気の方でした。

Kōzoku ni narareru mae kara mo kedakai fun'iki no kata deshita.

There was a noble air about her even before she became a member of the Imperial family.

kehai 気配 sign of *ki*

■ an indication, a sign

❏ 部屋は真っ暗だったが誰かいる気配がした。

Heya wa makkura datta ga dare ka iru kehai ga shita.

The room was pitch black, but I sensed (felt) that someone was there.

❏ 電気はついているのに家の中に人のいる気配が全くないね。

Denki wa tsuite iru no ni uchi no naka ni hito no iru kehai ga mattaku nai ne.

The lights are on, but there's no indication at all that anybody's home.

❏ 2階で何か動く気配がしなかったかい。

Nikai de nanika ugoku kehai ga shinakatta kai.

Did you hear something move upstairs?

Not to be confused with 気配り *kikubari*.

---

genki 元気 original *ki*

■ energy, vitality; (good) health

❏ シロが最近元気がないので心配だ。

Shiro ga saikin genki ga nai no de shinpai da.

I've been a little worried the way Shiro [a dog] has been moping around lately.

❏ なんとなく元気が出ないよ。

Nan to naku genki ga denai yo.

I just don't seem to have any energy.

❏ 子供たちは元気いっぱい踊った。

Kodomo-tachi wa genki ippai odotta.
The children danced energetically.

❑ そんな顔しないで、もっと元気を出して。
Sonna kao shinai de, motto genki o dashite.
Don't look so glum. Cheer up!

❑ 山田さんを元気づけるためにみんなで飲みに行こう。
Yamada-san o genki-zukeru tame ni minna de nomi ni ikō.
Let's all go out for a drink to cheer Yamada up.

❑ 今日は、悟ずいぶん元気がいいなあ。
Kyō wa, Satoru zuibun genki ga ii nā.
Hey Satoru, you're sure bright-eyed and bushy-tailed (full of vim and vigor) today.

❑ これ飲んでごらんよ、元気がつくから。
Kore nonde goran yo, genki ga tsuku kara.
Take this. It'll make you feel better.

❑ さ、みんな、外へ出て元気よく遊ぼう。
Sa, minna, soto e dete genki yoku asobō.
All right, everybody, it's time to go out and play. [A teacher to his pupils.]

❑ お元気でお過ごしのご様子、お喜び申し上げます。
Ogenki de osugoshi no goyōsu, oyorokobi mōshi agemasu.
I'm happy to hear you are well. [In a somewhat formal letter.]

➥genki (na) 元気(な) original *ki*
■ active, cheerful, energetic, lively

❑ 皆様お元気ですか。
Mina-sama ogenki desu ka. [in a letter]
How is everyone?

❑ いつも元気なぼうやねえ。
Itsumo genki na bōya nē.
You're a cheerful little fella, aren't you.

❑ じゃ、みなさん、名前を呼ばれたら元気にお返事しましょうね。
Ja, mina-san, namae o yobaretara genki ni ohenji shimashō ne.
OK, everybody, when I call your name, I want you to answer in a loud voice.

samuke 寒気 cold *ki*

■ a chill, shudder; the chills, shivers

❑ 寒気がするから、今日は風邪薬飲んで早く寝よう。

Samuke ga suru kara, kyō wa kaze-gusuri nonde hayaku neyō.

I've got the chills, so I think I'll take some cold medicine and get to bed early.

❑ 少し熱でもあるらしく、寒気を覚えた。

Sukoshi netsu de mo aru rashiku, samuke o oboeta.

I think I might have come down with a bit of a fever. I've got the shivers.

❑ そんな恐ろしいこと思っただけでも寒気がするよ。

Sonna osoroshii koto omotta dake de mo samuke ga suru yo.

It's so horrible it makes me shudder just to think of it.

➡samukedatsu 寒気立つ cold *ki* stands

■ get a chill, shudder

❑ その事件の全貌が明らかになるにつれ、同じ年頃の子を持つ親は寒気立ったに違いない。

Sono jiken no zenbō ga akiraka ni naru ni tsure, onaji toshigoro no ko o motsu oya wa samukedatta ni chigai nai.

Parents with children around the same age must have felt a cold chill (gotten a scare) as the details of the crime took shape.

❑ 暖かい日が続いてたが、今朝は久々に寒気立つなあ。

Atatakai hi ga tsuzuite ita ga, kesa wa hisabisa ni samukedatsu nā.

We've had a little warm spell here lately, but it's a bit chilly (there's a chill in the air) this morning.

Another of those pesky multiple readings/meanings. The characters 寒気 can also be read *kanki*, which is strictly a meteorological term for "cold air."

➤ 日本列島はすっぽり寒気に覆われていて、今日も寒い一日になりそうです。

Nihon-rettō wa suppori kanki ni ōwarete ite, kyō mo samui ichinichi ni narisō desu.

Japan (the Japanese archipelago) is covered by a cold air mass, so we can look forward to yet another cold day today.

shōki 正気 right *ki*

1. sanity, right-mindedness, all there

❑ 心配するな。俺は正気だ。

Shinpai suru na. Ore wa shōki da.

Don't worry. I know what I'm doing.

❑ 自分で正気だという奴に限って正気じゃないそうだよ。

Jibun de shōki da to iu yatsu ni kagitte shōki ja nai sō da yo.

I've heard that it's the guys who think they're all there that really aren't (who are really out of their senses).

❐ 麻薬で一時的に正気を失っていたということだ。

Mayaku de ichiji-teki ni shōki o ushinatte ita to iu koto da.

It's a case of someone flipping out for a while because he's on drugs.

❐ 兄貴のやってることはとても正気の沙汰じゃない。

Aniki no yatte 'ru koto wa totemo shōki no sata ja nai.

You've gone completely off the deep end.

❐ お前あの女に騙されてるんだぞ。正気に返れ。

Omae ano onna ni damasarete 'ru n' da zo. Shōki ni kaere.

You'd better come to your senses (wake up); the girl's sleeping around on you.

❐ 正気を取り戻すまでは誰が何を言っても聞く耳は持たんでしょう。

Shōki o torimodosu made wa dare ga nani o itte mo kiku mimi wa motan deshō.

He's not going to listen to anything anybody says until he's regained his senses.

❐ 正気になって考えると、どうしてあんなインチキ話にひっかかったのか自分でも不思議さ。

Shōki ni natte kangaeru to, dōshite anna inchiki-banashi ni hikkakatta no ka jibun de mo fushigi sa.

When I came to my senses and thought about it, I couldn't understand how I could have ever fallen for such a lamebrain scheme.

   ☞ *ki ga tashika (na)* 気が確か(な)

   ☛ *kyōki* 狂気, *ki ga kuruu* 気が狂う, *ki ga chigau* 気が違う, *ki ga fureru* 気がふれる, *ki ga hen ni naru* 気が変になる

2. consciousness

❐ 正気に返ったら、財布も時計もなくなってたんです。

Shōki ni kaettara, saifu mo tokei mo nakunatte 'ta n' desu.

When I came to (around), my wallet and watch were both gone.

❐ 事故から丸一日たってやっと正気を取り戻したんだ。

Jiko kara maru-ichinichi tatte yatto shōki o torimodoshita n' da.

It took him a full day to regain consciousness after the accident.

sono ki その気 that ki

■ the mood, feeling

❐ 一度はその気になったんだが、結局気が変わった。

Ichido wa sono ki ni natta n' da ga, kekkyoku ki ga kawatta.

I was ready to do it at one time, but I've changed my mind.

❐ 若い頃は政治家になる気はなかったが、中年になってその気になっ
た。

*Wakai koro wa seiji-ka ni naru ki wa nakatta ga, chūnen ni natte sono ki
ni natta.*

I had no thought of going into politics when I was young, but middle age
changed all that.

❐ 一杯やって行こうと誘われたが、今日はその気にならなかった。

Ippai yatte ikō to sasowareta ga, kyō wa sono ki ni naranakatta.

They invited me to go out with them for a drink, but today I just didn't
feel like it.

❐ その気があるのなら早く言った方がいいよ。

Sono ki ga aru no nara hayaku itta hō ga ii yo.

If that's the way you feel, you'd better go ahead and say so.

❐ 前々から言われてはいるが、まだその気はない。

Maemae kara iwarete wa iru ga, mada sono ki wa nai.

Everybody's been trying to talk me into it, but I just don't feel like doing
it.

❐ 彼はいつもその気だ。

Kare wa itsumo sono ki da.

He's horny all the time. / He's always ready to go.

❐ その気にさせておいて、今になって逃げるなんてひどいよ。

Sono ki ni sasete oite, ima ni natte nigeru nante hidoi yo.

How can you get me in the mood like that and then just up and take off?

Ambiguity at its best. Structurally, *sono ki* fits the same mold as the
entries listed under section one of the ~ *ki* heading, *sono* replacing the
verb normally in that position, often to avoid repeating it (see the note
under ~ *ki*). Although the expresson itself is ambiguous, just what the
sono means is usually clear from the context, especially from what has
preceded. Of all the possible meanings, however, the one most readily
understood without reference to context is euphemistic mention of
sexual excitement. *Sono ki* is the kind of expression likely to be picked
up and commented upon, often with a wink and a nudge, even when the
speaker intends no sexual innuendo. Relatedly—broadly speaking—is
another pronunciation of the term, *sono ke,* which in context is a slang
term describing someone of abnormal or unusual sexual tendencies.

➤ お前その気があるんじゃないか。

Omae sono ke ga aru n' ja nai ka.

What are you, queer or what?

❑ あの人その気があるみたいよ。
Ano hito sono ke ga aru mitai yo.
You can tell he's into S&M.

sonna ki　そんな気　that (kind of) *ki*

■ that feeling, (feel) that way, feel like

❑ そんな気はなかったんだが、どうも誤解されちゃったみたいなんだよ。
Sonna ki wa nakatta n' da ga, dōmo gokai sarechatta mitai nan da yo.
That's not what I had in mind at all. It looks like they took it the wrong way.

❑ そう言われればそんな気もする。
Sō iwarereba sonna ki mo suru.
Now that you mention it, that's probably right.

❑ パーティーに誘われたけど、とてもそんな気になれないよ。
Pātī ni sasowareta kedo, totemo sonna ki ni narenai yo.
I was invited to a party, but I'm not in the mood (in the party mode) at all.

As with *sono ki,* its linguistic cousin, *sonna ki* fits the same mold as a class of entry—#2—listed under the ~ *ki* heading, with *sonna* replacing the part of speech normally in that position, often to avoid repeating it (see the note under ~ *ki*). Although the expression itself is ambiguous, its meaning is usually clear from the context. See the examples below to get a clearer picture of the difference between the two expressions in the same context:

➤ そちらがその気なら、こちらにも考えがある。
Sochira ga sono ki nara, kochira ni mo kangae ga aru.
If that's what you're up to, I've got a little something up my sleeve as well.

➤ そちらがそんな気なら、こちらにも考えがある。
Sochira ga sonna ki nara, kochira ni mo kangae ga aru.
If that's the way you feel, don't expect much help from me.

nanige nai　何気ない　no *ki* at all

■ casual, cool, indifferent, nonchalant

❑ 何気ない仕草の端々に品のよさが感じられる人ですね。

Nanige nai shigusa no hashibashi ni hin no yosa ga kanjirareru hito desu ne.

She's a woman whose excellect upbringing shows in all the nonchalant little gestures she makes.

❒ 彼の何気ない一言がヒントになったよ。
Kare no nanige nai hitokoto ga hinto ni natta yo.
Some casual comment he made gave me a hint.

➡nanige naku 何気なく without *ki*

■ as though it were nothing, coolly, indifferently, nonchalantly; thoughtlessly, without thinking

❒ 何気なく窓の外を見ると夕焼けがきれいだった。
Nanige naku mado no soto o miru to yūyake ga kirei datta.
I kinda just looked outside, and boy was there a beautiful sunset.

❒ 何気なく言ったことが彼女を傷つけてしまったらしいんだよ。
Nanige naku itta koto ga kanojo o kizutsukete shimatta rashii n' da yo.
Some offhand comment I made seems to have hurt her.

⇨ *nan no ki nashi ni* 何の気なしに, *futo* ふと

namaiki (na) 生意気(な) fresh *ki*

■ cheeky, fresh, impertinent, insolent

❒ 新入りのくせに生意気なことを言うな。
Shin'iri no kuse ni namaiki na koto o iu na.
For a new guy you're a real smart-ass.

❒ 息子は近ごろ生意気になって口答えばかりするんですよ。
Musuko wa chikagoro namaiki ni natte kuchigotae bakari suru n' desu yo.
My son's become a little wise guy, always talking back.

ninki 人気 people's *ki*

■ popularity, [～の] fashionable, in, in vogue, popular, trendy

❒ あの新人候補は人気だけでトップ当選した。
Ano shinjin-kōho wa ninki dake de toppu-tōsen shita.
That new candidate got the most votes during the election on the sole strength of her popularity.

❒ このゲームの爆発的人気の理由は何だろうか。
Kono gēmu no bakuhatsu-teki ninki no riyū wa nan darō ka.
What do you suppose is behind this game's explosive popularity?

❑ 人気のランチスペシャルは試してみる価値があるよ。

Ninki no ranchi-supesharu wa tameshite miru kachi ga aru yo.

The popular lunch special is well worth a try.

❑ 若い人の間で人気のディスコが近くにあるけど、行ってみる？

Wakai hito no aida de ninki no disuko ga chikaku ni aru kedo, itte miru?

There's a disco nearby that's popular (that's in) with the young crowd. Wanna check it out?

❑ ボディ・ピアスは最近急に人気が出てきた。

Bodī-piasu wa saikin kyū ni ninki ga dete kita.

Body piercing is suddenly all the rage.

❑ 最近また和服の人気が出てきたそうだ。

Saikin mata wafuku no ninki ga dete kita sō da.

Recently, they're saying kimonos are getting popular again.

❑ いつまでも今の人気が続くとは思えない。

Itsu made mo ima no ninki ga tsuzuku to wa omoenai.

I can't see it staying as popular as it is now forever.

❑ 恐竜は子供の間でいつの時代も変わらない人気を保ち続けている。

Kyōryū wa kodomo-tachi no aida de itsu no jidai mo kawaranai ninki o tamochitsuzukete iru.

Dinosaurs have continued to maintain their popularity with kids over the years.

❑ 芸名を変えたとたんに人気が落ちちゃった。

Geimei o kaeta totan ni ninki ga ochichatta.

His popularity plummeted the instant he changed his stage name.

❑ クリスティの『ねずみとり』は初演以来大人気で、これまで40年以上連続公演されている。

Kurisutī no "Nezumi-tori" wa shoen irai dai-ninki de, kore made yonjū-nen ijō renzoku kōen sarete iru.

Agatha Christie's *Mousetrap* has been a big hit, performed continuously since its opening more than forty years ago.

❑ Ｊリーグが発足してサッカーは大人気だから、試合の切符がなかなか手に入らない。

Jē-rīgu ga hossoku shite sakkā wa dai-ninki da kara, shiai no kippu ga nakanaka te ni hairanai.

Soccer's taken the nation by storm since the J-League started up, so tickets are nearly impossible to come by.

➡ninki ga aru 人気がある

■ be all the rage, in, popular; enjoy popularity

❑ この雑誌はもともと若い人向けだったが、今ではむしろ中年の人の間で人気がある。

Kono zasshi wa motomoto wakai hito muke datta ga, ima de wa mushiro chūnen no hito no aida de ninki ga aru.

This magazine originally targeted younger readers, but has ended up being popular among middle-aged people instead.

❐ 人気のある時はいいが、落ち目になったらみじめだよ。

Ninki no aru toki wa ii ga, ochime ni nattara mijime da yo.

Everything's hunky-dory when you're hot, but it's really the pits when you start going downhill.

❐ 少し人気があると思って天狗になっているんじゃないか。

Sukoshi ninki ga aru to omotte tengu ni natte irun ja nai ka.

Look at you! Get the least bit popular, and it goes straight to your head.

➡ninki ga nai 人気がない

■ be out, unpopular

❐ どこといって悪いところはないのになぜか人気がない。

Doko to itte warui tokoro wa nai no ni naze ka ninki ga nai.

There's nothing in particular that's wrong with him, but for some reason no one seems to like him.

❐ 売り場面積が狭いので、人気のない商品はどんどん入れ換えている。

Uriba-menseki ga semai no de, ninki no nai shōhin wa dondon irekaete iru.

The shop's floor space is limited, so we're always changing the displays to get rid of products that don't sell (aren't moving, popular).

➡ninki + noun 人気＋名詞

■ popular [The following examples are given to show the variety of nouns used in this construction.]

❐ うちの祐二はクラスの人気者だ。

Uchi no Yūji wa kurasu no ninki-mono da.

My Yuji's one of the most popular kids in his class.

❐ この動物園の人気者はなんといってもパンダとラッコでしょう。

Kono dōbutsu-en no ninki-mono wa nan to itte mo panda to rakko deshō.

Two of the most popular animals in the zoo are almost certainly the panda and the otter.

❐ 処女作を発表してすぐ人気作家になった。

Shojo-saku o happyō shite sugu ninki-sakka ni natta.

He became a best-selling author soon after publishing his first book.

❐ 週刊誌はまたも人気力士と人気女優の婚約の話題でもちきりだ。

Shūkan-shi wa mata mo ninki-rikishi to ninki-joyū no kon'yaku no wadai de mochikiri da.

Once again the weeklies are full of stories about another engagement between a popular sumo wrestler and a popular actress.

❑ 人気選手が必ずしもチームにいちばん貢献しているわけではない。

Ninki-senshu ga kanarazushimo chīmu ni ichiban kōken shite iru wake de wa nai.

The popular ball players aren't necessarily the ones who contribute the most to the team.

❑ この歌は人気ドラマの主題歌として有名になった。

Kono uta wa ninki-dorama no shudai-ka toshite yūmei ni natta.

This song became famous as the theme song for a popular TV soap.

❑ 冷やし中華は夏の人気メニューだ。

Hiyashi-chūka wa natsu no ninki-menyū da.

Cold Chinese-style noodles are a popular summer dish.

How do you read 人気? Well, you know there have to be at least two ways for us to ask the question, right? And since you've read the entry to here, you probably know how to use the first and most common, *ninki* (popularity). The key to figuring out whether it's that reading or the other, *hitoke* (a sign or sense of someone being around), is, of course, the context and, more helpfully, the phrase in which it appears. *Ninki* is the only reading when the word is followed by ~ *ga deru,* ~ *ga ochiru,* ~ *ga ochime,* and ~ *ga takai,* most of which are exemplified above, or preceded by the likes of *sugoi , batsugun no, saikō no,* and *takai. Hitoke,* on the other hand, does not appear outside a very limited number of expressions: ~ *ga (no, mo) aru,* ~ *ga (no, mo) nai,* ~ *ga (no) ōi* and ~ *ga (no) sukunai.*

Having read through the above entry, those slightly ahead of the game will wonder about the several situations in which either reading is possible, namely ~ *ga (no, mo) aru* and ~ *ga (no, mo) nai.* The short answer is, "good luck," because it all depends on what is being discussed. Take 人気のない寂しい裏通り, for example. It could be *ninki,* I guess, but why would anyone be talking about whether a back alley was popular or not? And why would they use the adjective *sabishii* (lonesome or empty) about it? No, it's *hitoke.* Of course, the contrarians among us will be quick to point out that if it's not popular, *ninki ga nai,* then there sure won't be any people milling around (*hitoke ga nai*) and likewise if there's no sign of anyone being around, well then it certainly isn't a popular place, not at that moment at least.

One final note, in case you haven't realized it, 大人気 also has two unrelated readings. One, *dai-ninki,* shows up in two examples above; the other, *otonage,* is embedded in the entry *otonage (ga) nai,* to which an explanatory note similar to the one above is attached.

---

nemuke 眠気 sleepy *ki*

■ drowsiness, sleepiness

❑ 丘の上から見たその村の風景は眠気を誘うように穏やかだった。

Oka no ue kara mita sono mura no fūkei wa nemuke o sasou yō ni oda-yaka datta.

The view of the sleepy village from the top of the hill was so peaceful.

❑ 映画の途中で急に眠気に襲われて居眠りしちまったよ。

Eiga no tochū de kyū ni nemuke ni osowarete inemuri shichimatta yo.

I got so sleepy (I just couldn't keep my eyes open) during the movie and ended up nodding off in the middle of it.

❑ 運転中眠気を催したら、無理せず、車を止めて仮眠するとよい。

Unten-chū nemuke o moyōshitara, muri sezu, kuruma o tomete kamin suru to yoi.

If you get drowsy (get sleepy, start nodding off) when you're on the road, you ought to just pull over and take a nap.

❑ その知らせを聞いて眠気もすっ飛んだ。

Sono shirase o kiite nemuke mo suttonda.

I woke right up when I heard the news.

❑ 起きて2時間にもなるのにまだ眠気が覚めないよ。

Okite niji-kan ni mo naru no ni mada nemuke ga samenai yo.

I've been up for two hours and I'm still half asleep.

❑ 眠気を覚ますには冷たいシャワーが一番さ。

Nemuke o samasu ni wa tsumetai shawā ga ichiban sa.

Nothing like a cold shower to wake you right up.

➡nemukezamashi 眠気覚まし a sleepy *ki* wake-up

1: waking up; *something* used to wake *one* up

❑ まだボーッとしてるんでしょ。眠気覚ましにコーヒーをどうぞ。

Mada bōtto shite 'ru n' desho. Nemukezamashi ni kōhī o dōzo.

Hey, sleepyhead, how about a little coffee to wake you up?

❑ ついうとうとしちゃうよ。眠気覚ましにちょっと散歩して来よう。

Tsui uto-uto shichau yo. Nemukezamashi ni chotto sanpo shite koyō.

I'm falling asleep here. Think I'll go for a walk to wake up.

2. [as *nemukezamashi mitai na mon (koto)*] child's play; a cinch, cake-walk, picnic, piece of cake, snap

❑ この程度の仕事は彼にとっては眠気覚ましみたいなものさ。

Kono teido no shigoto wa kare ni totte wa nemukezamashi mitai na mono sa.

A little job like this is a piece of cake for him.

⇨ *asameshimae* 朝飯前, *he mitai na mono* 屁みたいなもの

nonki (na) 呑気(な), 暢気(な) loose *ki*

■ carefree, easy-going, laid-back, relaxed

❒ まったく何考えてるのか。呑気なんだから。

Mattaku nani kangaete 'ru no ka. Nonki nan da kara.

What are you thinking? Jeez, you're so happy-go-lucky!

❒ こっちは貧乏暇なしなのに、お前は呑気な身分で羨ましいよ。

Kotchi wa binbō hima nashi na no ni, omae wa nonki na mibun de urayamashii yo.

I sure envy you. Here I am working my buns off for peanuts while you kick back and take it all in.

Bear in mind that in a society that so respects and encourages industriousness, it is not always complimentary to be considered *nonki*.

☞ *kiraku (na)* 気楽(な) (see under *ki ga raku ni naru* 気が楽になる)

hakike 吐き気 vomiting *ki*

■ nausea, feeling sick to *one's* stomach

❒ 薬の副作用からか、ひどい吐き気におそわれた。

Kusuri no fuku-sayō kara ka, hidoi hakike ni osowareta.

I don't know if it was the medicine I took or what, but I started feeling sick to my stomach.

❒ 乗り物酔いで吐き気がする。

Norimono-yoi de hakike ga suru.

I feel carsick.

❒ 食べ物を見ただけで吐き気を催すんです。

Tabemono o mita dake de hakike o moyōsu n' desu.

Just the sight of food turns my stomach.

❒ これでも音楽かよ。吐き気がするぜ。

Kore de mo ongaku ka yo. Hakike ga suru ze.

You call this music? Makes me wanna barf (blow chunks).

❒ 昨日見たホラー映画は吐き気を催すような場面の連続で、途中でやめたよ。

Kinō mita horā-eiga wa hakike o moyōsu yō na bamen no renzoku de, tochū de yameta yo.

There were so many gory scenes in the horror flick I went to yesterday that I left halfway through.

hitoke 人気 people's *ki*

■ a sign that *someone* is around; [~ *ga nai*] unpopulated, empty, not a sign of anyone

❑ 屋台を出すなら、もっと人気がある所にすればいいのに。

Yatai o dasu nara, motto hitoke no aru tokoro ni sureba ii no ni.

If you're going to set up a stall to sell food, wouldn't it be better to do it in a place where there are more people around?

❑ 旅館の裏手は人気もなく、広間の宴会の音も聞こえなかった。

Ryokan no urate wa hitoke mo naku, hiroma no enkai no oto mo kikoe-nakatta.

There wasn't anybody around in the rear of the inn, and you couldn't even hear the party being held in the banquet room.

❑ この公園は夜になると人気がなくなるから、女の人は一人で歩かない方がいいのよ。

Kono kōen wa yoru ni naru to hitoke ga nakunaru kara, onna no hito wa hitori de arukanai hō ga ii no yo.

There aren't many people in the park after dark, so it's probably not a good idea for a woman to go there alone.

Almost always appears in the negative. See note at *ninki* for tips on when the characters are read as *hitoke* or *ninki*.

---

byōki 病気 sick *ki*

1. (a) condition, a disease, sickness; (an) illness,

❑ 父が心臓の病気で先日入院しましてね。

Chichi ga shinzō no byōki de senjitsu nyūin shimashite ne.

Yeah, Dad went into the hospital the other day for a heart condition. / My father was hospitalized the other day with heart disease.

❑ 彼の病気はかなり重いようで、心配なんですが。

Kare no byōki wa kanari omoi yō de, shinpai nan desu ga.

He appears to be quite seriously ill, and it has me worried (we're worried).

❑ 病気が直ったらまた一緒に山へ行こうよ。

Byōki ga naottara mata issho ni yama e ikō yo.

Let's go hiking again once you get better (recover, get over your illness).

❑ 毎日そんなに飲んでるとしまいには病気になるよ。

Mainichi sonna ni nonde 'ru to shimai ni wa byōki ni naru yo.

Keep drinking like that and you'll end up sick.

❑ この病気にかかったら、とにかく安静にしていることですね。

Kono byōki ni kakattara, tonikaku ansei ni shite iru koto desu ne.

Rest is the most important thing when you come down with this sickness.

❑ 病気の人は悲観的になりがちだから、気をつけてあげなくちゃ。

Byōki no hito wa hikan-teki ni narigachi da kara, ki o tsukete agena-kucha.

Sick people can quickly become pessimistic, so you've got to keep an eye on them.

❑ 病気の時はお互い様なんだから、遠慮しないで。

Byōki no toki wa otagaisama nan da kara, enryo shinai de.

Everybody gets sick sometime, so don't hesitate to ask for something if you need it.

❑ 変な病気うつされたんじゃないでしょうね。

Hen na byōki utsusareta n' ja nai deshō ne.

You didn't, like, catch something [from him/her], did you? [While *hen na byōki* may mean "a strange or unusual disease," it is also common slang for venereal disease, as is *myō na byōki*.]

❑ 悪い病気でなければいいんですが。

Warui byōki de nakereba ii n' desu ga.

I hope it's not the big C. [*Warui byōki* is often a euphemism for "cancer."]

❑ あいつほとんどビョーキだぜ。

Aitsu hotondo byōki da ze.

Dude's sick [in the head] (waaaaaay out there), man. [*Byōki* written in katakana, this trendy usage has yet to stand the test of time.]

In Japanese, an illness is commonly described as being either *karui* 軽い (slight, not serious; literally "light") or *omoi* 重い (serious; literally "heavy"). *Byōki ni naru* is used about about any disease, illness or sickness, while use of *byōki ni kakaru* is reserved for contagious diseases.

---

2. [of a bad habit or shortcoming] *one's* old tricks

❑ あいつ例の病気がぶり返したんじゃないか。

Aitsu rei no byōki ga burikaeshita n' ja nai ka.

I see he's up to his old tricks again.

❑ また悪い病気が始まったら、臭い飯を食うことになるぞ。

Mata warui byōki ga hajimattara, kusai meishi o kuu koto ni naru zo.

Start up again and you'll end up behind bars.

heiki (na) 平気(な) undisturbed *ki*

1. don't care, indifferent, insensitive; [*heiki de ~ o suru*] make no bones about *doing,* be unconcerned; nonchalance, calmness, unpreturbedness

❏ ゆうべのことなどなかったかのように平気な顔をしている。
Yūbe no koto nado nakatta ka no yō ni heiki na kao o shite iru.
She's acting as if nothing happened at all last night.

❏ 人気のない暗い道だって平気で歩けるわよ。
Hitoke no nai kurai michi datte heiki de arukeru wa yo.
I don't think anything of walking down dark, deserted streets.

❏ 何度注意しても平気な顔してまた遅れてくるんだよ。
Nando chūi shite mo heiki na kao shite mata okurete kuru n' da yo.
You can chew him out all you want; he still turns up late with a couldn't-care-less look on his face.

❏ レバーは平気だけどモツはだめなんだ。
Rebā wa heiki da kedo motsu wa dame nan da.
Liver doesn't bother me (I don't mind liver), but the guts, now, they're a different story.

❏ 「禁煙」の張り紙の前で平気でタバコを吸っている。
"Kin'en" no harigami no mae de heiki de tabako o sutte iru.
Guy's puffing away right in front of the "no smoking" sign like it wasn't even there!

2. without effect, without feeling a thing

❏ 僕は水割り2杯までなら平気だけど。
Boku wa mizuwari nihai made nara heiki da kedo.
I can handle a couple whisky-and-waters without any problem, but more than that and …

❏ このビルは関東大震災並みの地震が起こっても平気なんだってさ。
Kono biru wa Kantō-daishinsai nami no jishin ga okotte mo heiki nan datte sa.
They say this building can take an earthquake as strong as the Great Kanto Earthquake, no sweat.

❏ 慣れると平気になってしまうらしいね。
Nareru to heiki ni natte shimau rashii ne.
You'll get over it once you get used to it. / Once you get used to it, apparently it's no big deal.

❏ あんなもの見た後で平気でいられるわけないだろう。
Anna mono mita ato de heiki de irareru wake nai darō.
After seeing something like that, you can hardly expect me to act the

same as always.

➡heiki no heiza 平気の平左

■ cool as a cucumber, unflappable

❏ 大丈夫だよ、僕は何を言われても平気の平左だから。

Daijōbu da yo, boku wa nani o iwarete mo heiki no heiza da kara.

Don't worry about me, I'm Mr. Cool. I don't give a hoot what people say.

  ☞ *ki ni shinai* 気にしない (see under *ki ni suru* 気にする)

honki 本気 real *ki*

■ earnestness, seriousness, sincerity; no fooling, for real

❏ みんなは信じていないが、彼は本気なんですよ。

Minna wa shinjite inai ga, kare wa honki nan desu yo.

No one believes him, but he's not playing around (he's serious).

❏ 私は正気じゃないかも知れないが、本気だ。

Watashi wa shōki ja nai kamo shirenai ga, honki da.

I may not be sane (in my right mind), but I am serious.

❏ 会社をやめて田舎へ帰るって聞いたんだが、本気なのか？

Kaisha o yamete inaka e kaeru tte kiita n' da ga, honki na no ka?

I heard you were quitting work and going back to your hometown. Are you serious?

❏ 君が本気なら私もできるだけのお手伝いはしよう。

Kimi ga honki nara watashi mo dekiru dake no otetsudai wa shiyō.

If you mean what you say, I'll do what I can to help.

➡honki de ~ o suru 本気で～をする to do ~ with real *ki*

■ be serious about *something,* get behind *something*

❏ 本気で販売戦略を展開すれば絶対売れるはずだ。

Honki de hanbai-senryaku o tenkai sureba zettai ureru hazu da.

If we throw ourselves into the sales strategy, I know the product will move.

❏ 政府は本気で流通の規制緩和を進める構えだ。

Seifu wa honki de ryūtsū no kisei-kanwa o susumeru kamae da.

The government appears to be serious about relaxing distribution regulations.

❏ 本気でやりさえすれば1日でできる仕事だ。

Honki de yari sae sureba ichinichi de dekiru shigoto da.

Get serious about it, and you can polish the job off in a day.

❏ 僕は君のことを本気で心配しているんだよ。

Boku wa kimi no koto o honki de shinpai shite iru n' da yo.
In all seriousness (No kidding), I'm worried about you.

➡honki ni naru 本気になる to become real *ki*

■ get serious, get down to business, get down to it

本気になればもっと成績が上がるのは確かなんだけどねえ。
Honki ni nareba motto seiseki ga agaru no wa tashika nan da kedo nē.
I know she could get better grades if she just buckled down (got serious).

❒ 迷いに迷ったが、やっと本気になった。
Mayoi ni mayotta ga, yatto honki ni natta.
I might have fooled around for a long time, but I now I'm ready to get down to business.

❒ もっと本気になって聞いて下さい。
Motto honki ni natte kiite kudasai.
Listen to what I'm saying, would you.

❒ うちのやつが本気になって怒り出すと怖いぞ。
Uchi no yatsu ga honki ni natte okoridasu to kowai zo.
It's scary as hell when the old lady really gets pissed off (flies into a rage, flies off the handle).

➡honki ni suru 本気にする to make into real *ki*

■ take *someone* seriously, take *someone* at his word

❒ 本気にするかどうかは君次第だが、僕は嘘はついていない。
Honki ni suru ka dō ka wa kimi shidai da ga, boku wa uso wa tsuite inai.
It's up to you whether you take me at my word, but I'm not just talking through my hat.

❒ 子供達ははじめは父の言うことを本気にしなかった。
Kodomo-tachi wa hajime wa chichi no iu koto o honki ni shinakatta.
The kids didn't believe their father at first.

❒ そういう冗談をいちいち本気にしていたら身が持たないぞ。
Sō iu jōdan o ichi-ichi honki ni shite itara mi ga motanai zo.
If you take every little joke seriously, you'll screw yourself up.

yamai wa ki kara 病は気から illness comes from *ki*

■ the mind rules the body, no sickness is completely physical

❒ 「病は気から」というが、あの人も奥さんを亡くしてからすっかり落ち込んで病気がちになってしまった。
"Yamai wa ki kara" to iu ga, ano hito mo okusan o nakushite kara suk-kari ochikonde byōki-gachi ni natte shimatta.
He's a living example of what they say about the mind ruling the body; he's been depressed and sickly ever since he lost his wife.

❒ 「病は気から」ですよ。そんな暗い顔してちゃ治るものも治りゃしない。元気出して。

"Yamai wa ki kara" desu yo. Sonna kurai kao shite 'cha naoru mono mo naorya shinai. Genki dashite.

Remember, "Mind over matter." Walking around with a long face like that's not going to help anything. Cheer up.

Can be used to cheer up an ill person, though care must be taken to use it only if the illness is not too serious, for the implication is that since the ill person's attitude itself is causing his distress, it can't be all that bad. History bears this out. Upon visiting a hospital for atomic bomb victims in Hiroshima, one former Japanese prime minister caused quite an uproar when he thoughtlessly told one patient that it was "all a mental thing." Sure.

⇨ *ki karukereba yamai karushi* 気軽ければ病軽し

yaruki やる気 *ki* to do

■ ambition, desire, drive, enthusiasm, fight, get up and go, motivation, will

❒ やる気がある人だけに来てもらいたい。

Yaruki ga aru hito dake ni kite moraitai.

We want only motivated people.

❒ しょっちゅう遅刻するのはやる気のない証拠だ。

Shotchū chikoku suru no wa yaruki no nai shōko da.

Coming late all the time is proof that you're not into your work.

❒ やる気のない選手はスタメンからはずせ。

Yaruki no nai senshu wa sutamen kara hazuse.

Take everybody out of the starting lineup who's not ready to put out.

❒ 社長のワンマン経営のせいで若手の社員はすっかりやる気をなくしている。

Shachō no wanman-keiei no sei de wakate no shain wa sukkari yaruki o nakushite iru.

All the younger employees are losing their drive because the boss runs the company like a one-man show.

❒ 彼も早く立ち直って、やる気になってくれればいいんだが。

Kare mo hayaku tachinaotte, yaruki ni natte kurereba ii n' da ga.

Everything would be all right if he could pull himself out of his slump and get back into things.

❒ みんな、もっとやる気を出してがんばろうよ。

Minna, motto yaruki o dashite ganbarō yo.

Come on, you guys. Let's get with the program (get cracking).

❑ 成功するもしないも君のやる気次第だ。

Seikō suru mo shinai mo kimi no yaruki shidai da.

Whether or not you succeed depends entirely on how bad you want it.

❑ 給料は歩合制ですからやる気次第でいくらでも稼げますよ。

Kyūryō wa buai-sei desu kara yaruki shidai de ikura de mo kasegemasu yo.

You'll be working on commission, so how much you earn is entirely up to you.

❑ 賢一君もついにやる気を起こして、今では見違えるように張り切っている。

Ken'ichi-kun mo tsui ni yaruki o okoshite, ima de wa michigaeru yō ni harikitte iru.

Even old Kenichi is into it now. You ought to see him; he's a changed man.

❑ やる気が起きないってまさか鬱病の始まりじゃないだろうね。

Yaruki ga okinai tte masaka utsubyō no hajimari ja nai darō ne.

So you can't get interested in anything, huh? I hope you're not starting to get depressed.

❑ この前までやる気満々だったのに、一体どうしたんだろう。

Kono mae made yaruki manman datta no ni, ittai dō shita n' darō.

You were all fired up until just the other day. What went wrong?

yōki (na) 陽気(な) bright *ki*

■ bright, cheerful, happy, outgoing

❑ 君んちのお母さんて陽気な人なんだなあ。

Kimi n' 'chi no okāsan te yōki na hito nan da nā.

Boy, your mom sure is a cheerful person.

❑ 原田さん陽気だから一緒にいるとこっちまで楽しくなっちゃう。

Harada-san yōki da kara issho ni iru to kotchi made tanoshiku natchau.

Harada's such a happy-go-lucky guy that it sort of rubs off on you when you're around him.

❑ ぱっと陽気に騒いで嫌なことは忘れようぜ。

Patto yōki ni sawaide iya na koto wa wasureyō ze.

Hey, man, let's party down and forget all the bad shit.

☛ *inki (na)* 陰気(な)

warugi 悪気 bad *ki*

■ an evil intention; malice

❏ 小沢さんに悪気がないのは分かっているが、それでも腹が立つ。
Ozawa-san ni warugi ga nai no wa wakatte iru ga, sore de mo hara ga tatsu.
I realize Ozawa's intentions weren't bad, but it still makes me mad.

❏ 悪気はなかったんだが、ついうっかりして忘れてしまった。
Warugi wa nakatta n' da ga, tsui ukkari shite wasurete shimatta.
I didn't mean anything by it; it just completely slipped my mind.

❏ 悪気のない冗談のつもりが、あいつすっかり怒っちゃった。
Warugi no nai jōdan no tsumori ga, aitsu sukkari okotchatta.
I was just makin' a harmless joke, but he really exploded.

❏ 悪気のある男じゃないんだが、あの無神経さにはまいるよ。
Warugi no aru otoko ja nai n' da ga, ano mushinkei-sa ni wa mairu yo.
He doesn't try to be an asshole, it's just that he's so damn thoughtless.

Index